T.L. OSBORN

OSFO BOOKS

Soul Winning

ENLARGED REVISED FOR THIS GENERATION

A Classic on Biblical Christianity

BOOKS BY T.L. AND DAISY OSBORN

BELIEVERS IN ACTION—*Apostolic*
FIVE CHOICES FOR WOMEN WHO WIN
GOD'S LOVE PLAN
HEALING THE SICK—*A Living Classic*
HOW TO BE BORN AGAIN
NEW LIFE FOR WOMEN
RECEIVE MIRACLE HEALING
SOULWINNING—
A Classic on Biblical Christianity
THE BEST OF LIFE
THE GOOD LIFE—*A Mini-Bible School*
THE GOSPEL, ACCORDING TO T.L. & DAISY
THE MESSAGE THAT WORKS
THE POWER OF POSITIVE DESIRE
THE WOMAN BELIEVER
WHY?—*Tragedy Trauma Triumph*
WOMAN WITHOUT LIMITS
WOMEN & SELF-ESTEEM
YOU ARE GOD'S BEST

Most Osborn books and audio or video cassettes are available at quantity discounts for bulk purchases, to be used for gifts, resale, ministry outreaches, educational or other purposes.

Publisher

Address:

OSFO Publishers
(Or T.L. Osborn, or LaDonna Osborn)
P.O. Box 10, Tulsa, OK 74102 USA
TEL: 918 743-6231
FAX: 918 749-0339 E-Mail: OSFO@
www.OSBORN.ORG

Canada: Box 281, Adelaide St. Post Sta., T
England: Box 148, Birmingham B
(A Registered Charity)

First Printing 1963

evised and Enlarged Edition
ISBN 0-87943-091-5
pyright 2000 by T.L. Osborn
d in the United States of America

CONTENTS

DEDICATED

To THE MEMORY OF DAISY, my late companion and associate minister throughout more than a half-century of evangelism together in over seventy nations, who believed as I do that all human persons are created in God's image and therefore have infinite value and limitless potential for good, once they understand God's love for them and receive Jesus Christ as their savior and Lord.

Crusade photographs by
Daisy Washburn Osborn

T.L. Osborn

Introduction

THE MISSION OF JESUS is now the mission of believers. The passion of Christ is now expressed through His followers. The love that drove Him to the *cross* now drives us to the *lost*. He trusts you and me to continue His ministry.

Around the world, I have seen millions transformed by the concepts in this book. My father has given 56 years to practicing what he has written in these life-changing pages.

Sharing what Christ has done is the pinnacle of *Biblical Christianity*. Solomon said, *Withhold not good from them to whom it is due, when it is in the power of your hand to do it.*[Pr.3:27]

The value of his book deeply impresses me. It will enlighten you as to your dignity and vitality in God's design for your life. It will unveil for you a new self-discovery as God's partner. It will focus your world and reveal how much God believes in *you as His interpreter*. It will engender *a new love for life* and unveil *a new purpose for living*.

You and God are teammates among hurting people. After reading this book, you will never again *demean* the value of your words and actions; you will never *grow old* in spirit; you will never *burn out* in ministry; you will never be *bored* with life; you will never *lose your freshens*, your enthusiasm for touching and blessing others.

This *Classic on Biblical Christianity* is a burning *Torch of Truth* for millions of believers, gospel workers, Bible students, preachers, ministers, and national leaders throughout the world.

Biblical Christianity is ministering God's Love and Life in our despairing world. What the believer possesses is the greatest healing and lifting power on earth. It will cure any disease, lift anyone who has fallen, breathe life into anyone discouraged, and engender self-value in anyone who has been abused. It will bring peace, health, success and objectivity to anyone who embraces Christ.

These truths that my father has learned in his long years of world ministry are *yours* now. READ THEM AND L-I-V-E!

Bishop LaDonna Osborn

Preface

A PROMINENT SOULWINNER once said: "Let the cross be raised again at the center of the marketplace, as well as on the steeple of the church. Jesus was not crucified in a cathedral between two candles, but on a cross between two thieves, at the crossroads so cosmopolitan that they had to write His title in Hebrew and Latin and Greek.

"The Son of God was crucified at the kind of place where cynics talk smut, where thieves curse, and where soldiers gamble. Because that is where He died and since that is what He died about, that is where Christians can best share His message of love because that is what real Christianity is all about."

First Century Christians lived with a passion to share their witness of Christ. They did it in a daily house to house, face to face ministry.

Following the death of the first apostles, theological controversy finally extinguished the Christians' compassion for the *un*converted, and apostasy resulted. By the Fourth Century, the Dark Ages had begun and it was not until the Eighteenth Century that evangelism began to reappear.

It is amazing that personal witnessing, as First Century believers practiced it, has only been re-discovered in recent decades. Christians have evangelized the sanctuary, the classrooms and the pews. But only in recent decades has there begun to be a rebirth of evangelizing the *uncon-verted world, beyond the walls of the church sanctu-ary.*

Drew Graham, a reporter who was converted in one of Billy Graham's crusades in London, England, served on our publication staff. His life had been profoundly affected and he was eager to share Christ with others. After reading the first edition of this book, he wrote:

> "At a time when many churches were desperate for new ways to draw sinners into their sanctuaries, T.L. Osborn produced a *Classic on Biblical Christianity* titled *Soulwinning – Out Where The People Are.* The book is aimed at motivating Christians to share the gospel outside their church walls.

> "Osborn's book was sent, as a gift to more than a hundred and twenty-five thousand missionaries and national church leaders, pastors and evangelists around the world. There is scarcely a nation where this book has not gone and proven to be a pacesetter, inspiring a dynamic resurgence of personal evangelism that is expressed beyond the boundaries of church structure. *Soulwinning* has rekindled a fresh passion in the hearts of Christian believers

worldwide to share the love of Christ with the *un*converted world.

"Since the Osborns made that investment, there has been a constantly increasing number of soulwinning associations and of enthusiastic companies of believers—both men and women—who have been on the rise and on the go, carrying the gospel of Christ and His love out where the people live and play and work.

"After his first rallying call for *Soulwinning — Out Where The People Are*, T.L. wrote a sequel which he titled *Outside The Sanctuary*. It included studies shared by him and his wife, Dr. Daisy, with tens of thousands of national pastors and gospel workers in their crusade follow-up seminars worldwide.

"The Osborns believe that committed Christians will write the last glorious chapter of the *Church in action* as they rediscover First Century soulwinning principles and emulate their example by sharing Christ and His love with the *un*converted world."

Soulwinning — Out Where The People Are, has been acclaimed by pastors, missionaries, gospel workers and national church leaders worldwide. Now this revised and enlarged edition includes all of the material previously published in *Outside The Sanctuary*, and is completely updated for the new young generation in this 21st Century.

The concepts expressed in this book encourage communication between church *in*siders and world *out*siders—in homes and schools, in factories and markets, in parks and streets — out where humanity hurts most and where only Christ's love can heal.

There is nothing equal to the dignity and self-value of being part of God's plan, *sharing the gospel and winning souls* out amidst suffering human persons who need our witness, our touch, our ear, our attention.

The seed is the word of God.[Lu.8:11] *The field is the world.*[Mt.13:38] *We are laborers together with God.*[1Co.3:9] Jesus said, *As my Father has sent me, even so send I you.*[Jn.20:21] The apostle John said, *As he is, so are we in this world.*[1Jn.4:17] Paul said, *God has committed unto us the word [or ministry] of reconciliation. Now then we are ambassadors for Christ.*[2Co.5:19-20] And he added, *This is the wonderful news that...is now spreading all over the world. And [we] have the joy of telling it to others* [Col.1:23 LB]

T. L. Osborn

Chapter 1

Join This Chariot

THE IDEA OF SOULWINNING is graphically depicted by the evangelist Philip, a Bible-day Jesus-man, who shared information about Christ with a celebrity traveling to Ethiopia.[Ac.8:26-40] The fellow became a believer in the Lord Jesus right there on the public thoroughfare.

That is what happens when a Christian believer shares Christ with people in our hurting world, *out where they are.*

This is putting the gospel where it belongs—on main street, on the broad highways and boulevards of humanity, out in public places, on wheels, in action, into motion—hooking it up to transportation, mounting it on gospel cine-vans and cine-boats, speeding it on the wheels of modern technology, on multi-color web presses, on the spools of audio or video tape and of motion film, and on electronic wave lengths, the inter-net and e-mail.

This is putting the gospel within reach of the masses, where the poor can hear it as well as the rich, where both beggars and merchants, illiterates and intellectuals can receive God's message of love, of hope and of faith—out along the public traffic ways, via the mass media, where millions who might never visit a church can hear about Jesus and become believers, like the Ethiopian eunuch did. It is putting the gospel *out where the people are.*

God was speaking to all believers when he said to Philip: *Go join yourself to this chariot.*[Ac.8:29] He was saying, "Put the gospel witness on board every modern, mechanized, transistorized, energized chariot of action that is functioning in the main stream of society. Go out there to your world and share the life and message of Jesus Christ."

Paul said: *The same Good News that came to you is going out all over the world and changing lives everywhere.*[Col.1:6 LB]

Let's do like Paul said that he did: *Everywhere we go, we talk about Christ to all who will listen... This is our work, and we can do it only because Christ's mighty energy is at work within us.*[Col.1:28-29 LB]

Chapter 2

Let's Take A Journey

HOW WOULD YOU like to visit the Early Church? Would their lifestyle of soulwinning interest you? How do you think they functioned as a church? Who were the preachers? How many were witnesses? Which denomination was the largest or the most popular?

What is your personal concept of the Church in New Testament times? Could we follow its example? Or have times changed too much?

Let's take a journey in our minds and make a visit to the church at Ephesus. Let's imagine a conversation we might have:

"Good evening, Priscilla. We understand that you and your husband, Aquila, are members of the church here. Could we come in and visit for awhile?"

"Certainly. Come in," Aquila motions.

"If you don't mind, we would like for you to tell us about the soulwinning programs of the churches here in Asia Minor. We read that you have been members of the church at Corinth and at Rome, as well as this one here at Ephesus. You must be qualified to tell us about evangelism in the New Testament Church. If you don't mind, we'd like to visit your church while we're here."

"Sit down," invites Priscilla. "You're already in the church. It meets here in our home."

"Where Is Your Sanctuary"?

We ask: "Where is your church building?"

"What's a church building?" Aquila queries. "No, I guess we don't have one."

"Tell us, what are the believers doing to reach the city of Ephesus with the gospel?"

"We've already evangelized Ephesus. Every person in the city has received a gospel witness."

"What?"

"Yes. Is that unusual?"

"How did you do it? You don't have radio, television, or electronic communication. Did you organize big public evangelism meetings?"

"No. As you may have heard, we tried public meetings in this area, but many Christians were arrested and thrown in jail because of their witness that Christ has risen from the dead."

"Then how have you reached the city?"

"We've just gone to people, wherever they are, at work, or in their private homes, and we have given Christ's message to them. That's the way the believers evangelized Jerusalem.[Ac.5:42] They did it in a very short time. And the other churches in Asia Minor have followed their example."

"Does that idea work everywhere?"

The Method That Works

"Yes, I believe we can say that it does. There are so many converts that some of the pagan leaders are afraid that their own religions are in jeopardy.[Ac.19:27] When Paul left Ephesus for the last time, he really urged us to keep on witnessing of Christ, regardless of the cost, and to do it *publickly and from house to house.*"[Ac.20:20]

"Priscilla and Aquila, this is truly amazing to us! At this rate, there is no way to imagine how many people are going to hear the gospel of our Lord Jesus Christ."

"Oh, haven't you heard? We've already shared the good news with all of Asia Minor, witnessing to both Jews and Greeks."[Ac.19:10]

"That's not possible. You don't mean *everyone*."

"Yes, *everyone*."

"But that would include Damascus, Ephesus, dozens of large cities, as well as towns and villages and even the nomadic desert tribes. How long did it take the believers to reach all of these people?"

"Not long; twenty-four months to be exact.[Ac.19:10] The same thing is happening all across northern Africa and southern Europe. In fact, some of the believers have already reached as far west as Spain. We've even heard of some great island-nations far to the north. We're quite sure that some Christians are already reaching them."

"Well, what you two believers have told us is overwhelming. You have done more in one generation than we have done in a millennium!"

"That's strange," the couple remarked in amazement. "The job has been rather simple for us. We're sorry to hear that things have moved so slowly for you. Perhaps there's a better way for you to share the good news about Christ."

Chapter 3

The Case In Brief

HERE IS THE case for soulwinning:

1. *Non*-Christians do not go to church.

2. Our commission is to *preach the gospel to every creature*.^{Mk.16:15}

3. Since *un*believers do not go to church, then Christians must take the gospel to them wherever they are, *outside the walls of the church*.

This is what Christianity is all about. In the First Century Church, both leaders and laity were *daily in the temple and in every house. They ceased not to teach and preach Jesus Christ*.^{Ac.5:42}

They did it in the temple — *daily*.

They did it in the houses — *daily*.

And they evangelized their world.

Today church leaders and lay people who care about souls, are discovering new dimensions of evangelism ministries, new ways to launch new outreaches among the *unchurched.*

Around the world, there is rapid rediscovery of First Century Christianity — the concept that *every believer is a witness of Christ.* The *un*converted world may not be interested in what a preacher has to say, but they want to know if Christ can be real to an individual.

We are living in the greatest epoch of evangelism in the history of Christianity. It is because ordinary followers of Christ have rediscovered the master key to the success of the Early Church; they are going outside the walls of their sanctuaries, telling people how Christ has affected their lives.

Many churches have not emphasized the ministry potential of individual believers, and have not focused gospel action toward the *un*converted. But today ineffective concepts are giving way to new life in believers, and millions of souls are being won to Christ as a result.

Jesus said, *I am come that they might have life, and that they might have it more abundantly.*[Jn.10:10] Peter said, *We are his witnesses.*[Ac.5:32]

Chapter 4

The Heartbeat
Of Soulwinning

A GROUP OF Christian women gathered at their prayer meeting. Their guest speaker was an enthusiastic soulwinner. He overheard them discussing a disreputable woman in their neighborhood so he asked: "What are you doing to show the love of Christ to that lady?"

The group leader spoke up, "We're praying for her salvation every time we meet."

"Fine," the evangelist remarked. "But she'll go to hell if all you do is pray. Have you visited her? Have you shown God's love to her? Have you gone to visit her in her home?"

Christians often seem to want God's Spirit to carry the message of His love to lost and hurting people. But *believers* are the ones to share the gospel. Church members spend much of their prayer time urging God to do all of the things that He chose *them* to do—visiting the poor and needy,

23

comforting the feeble, blessing and providing for the destitute, encouraging those in prison, sustaining the weak, witnessing to unbelievers, etc.

How can God's Spirit communicate His message to human persons without a Christian to express Himself through? What can Jesus Christ do in any town or community without *a body* to function through?

When God visited humankind to *manifest* [1Ti.3:16] Himself to people, the Bible says, *The Word was made flesh, and dwelt among us.*[Jn.1:14] He came in a physical body. Paul said *God [came] in Christ, reconciling the world unto himself.*[2Co.5:19] God came to us on our human level and expressed Himself through the life and witness of a human person— His Son, in the form of flesh and blood.

After Christ was crucified, He returned in the form of the Holy Spirit to take up His abode in human beings as His temple.[1Co.6:19] The astounding and dynamic fact of Christianity is that every time a person receives Jesus Christ as Lord and savior, in that individual, *the living Word,* [the Son of God] *is made flesh and dwells among us* [again].[Jn.1:14]

Basics For Believers

Now, *we* are the church—*we* are Christ's body. I am the Church—*I* am Christ's body. We are His expression in our community today.

Christ ministers through people today the same as He ministered through a human person (His Son born of a virgin) over two thousand years ago. Today His body is the Church. The Church is you and it is me. *We* are His temple, His channel of expression now. Today we are His associates, His friends, His partners, His interpreters, His communicators, His transmitters.

For we are members of his body, of his flesh, and of his bones.[Ep.5:30] *So we, being many, are one body in Christ.*[Ro.12:5] *Now [we] are the body of Christ, and members in particular.*[1Co.12:27] The mystery of the Christian faith is — *Christ in you.*[Co.1:27]

Jesus taught His followers about the Holy Spirit saying, *He dwells with you, and shall be in you.*[Jn.14:17] He added, *I am in the Father, and you are in me, and I am in you.*[Jn.14:20] He compared this relationship to the way that limbs and branches of a tree or vine are integral to their source. *I am the vine, you are the branches...Abide in me, and I in you.*[Jn.15:4-5]

He said, *You are my friends.*[Jn.15:14] Then He emphasized, *You have not chosen me, but I have chosen you.*[Jn.15:16] He told His followers that the Holy Spirit would *receive of his and show it unto them.*[Jn.16:14] Then He repeated those words. *He shall take of mine, and shall shew it unto you.*[Jn.16:15]

Jesus said, *I am come that you might have life and that you might have it more abundantly.*[Jn.10:10] Then He explained its real essence: *This is life eternal, that you might know the only true God, and Jesus Christ, whom he has sent.*[Jn.17:3]

He prayed for His followers: *As you, Father, have sent me into the world, even so have I also sent them into the world...Father, you are **in** me, and I am **in** you,* and I pray *that they also may be one **in** us.*[Jn.17:18,21] He repeated this again in His prayer for us: *I **in** them, and you Father, **in** me, that they may be made perfect **in** one.*[Jn.17:23] Then He closed His prayer for us with the words: *I **in** them.*[Jn.17:26]

The great truth of authentic Christianity is the preeminent fact that Jesus Christ has so thoroughly redeemed us to God, that it is as though no sin had ever been committed to separate us from Him.[Is.59:2] We are reconciled to God.

We Are Redeemed
For God To Live In

We have been *redeemed...with the precious blood of Christ, as of a lamb without blemish and without spot.*[1Pe.1:18-19] *He loved us, and washed us from our sins in his own blood.*[Re.1:5] Why? *We were brought back to God by the death of his Son...and now we are his friends, and he is living **within** us.*[Ro.5:10LB]

That is the essence of biblical Christianity. God redeemed us so that now *He can live **within** us* and express Himself *through us.* Paul summarized the issue in three pivotal words: *Christ **in** you.*[Col.1:27] He added, *He works **in** us mightily.*[Col.1:29]

He said, *That Christ may dwell in your hearts by faith.*[Ep.3:17] *You are built for a **habitation** of God through the Spirit.*[Ep.2:22] He alerted us, *Know you not your own selves, how that Jesus Christ is in you.*[2Co.13:5] And John added, *Greater is he that is in you, than he that is in the world.*[1Jn.4:4]

Paul testified: *Christ lives in me.*[Ga.2:20] He said, *You are the **temple** of God, and the Spirit of God dwells in you…The temple of God is holy, which temple **you** are.*[1Co.3:16-17] *Your body is the **temple** of the Holy Ghost which is in you…For you are bought with a price.*[1Co.6:19-20] *You are the **temple** of the living God: God has said, I will dwell in you, and walk in you; and I will be your God and you shall be my people…I will be a Father unto you, and you shall be my sons and daughters.*[2Co.6:16,18]

You see why this truth is so significant to the Christian faith. *Our Lord can do nothing except through His body. He functions through you and me* — not our congregations or our denominations. *We* — you and me — *we* are Christ's body.

We Will Speak For Ourselves

When we stand before God, we will not be judged in the light of what our church congregation did as a corporate body of believers. God will not call our assembly as a unit for judgment. He will not judge what our particular church has accomplished. We will give an account of the deeds that we personally have done.[Mt.12:36]

We will not be able to say, "Lord, my pastor will speak for me. I am a faithful member of the church body. We all work as a unit so I cannot answer as an individual."

We are each, individually, *the Church* and we will each answer for our own thoughts, our words, and our actions.

Christians seem to feel more comfortable speaking of the body of Christ as the *mystical union or spiritual community of believers*—which the Church is. But like all truth, it must become personalized—it must put on flesh before it can bear fruit.

Christians often regard the body of Christ in its *collective*, rather than its *personal* sense. But salvation is not a collective experience; it is a personal experience. Christ Jesus lives within each individual believer.

This intimate relationship that we have been accorded through Christ, is what humanity has longed for throughout history, but could not experience, because of sin in the human race.

Jesus Christ—Our Vitality

Paul refers to our oneness with God as *the great mystery which has been hid from ages and from gen-*

erations, but now is made manifest to his [children]...*which is Christ in you.*[Col.1:26,27] The ransom has been paid by the blood of Christ to redeem us from the domination of sin. We have been reconciled to God and justified before Him so perfectly and completely that it is as though no sin had ever been committed.

That is why Jesus Christ can now come and *live in us and through us.* That is why we can now receive Him in our lives. That is why we have been made the *temple of the Holy Ghost* and have become His body in action. *In him we [now] live, and move, and have our being.*[Ac.17:28]

It sounds more plausible to say that we are members of his *corporate body* — and we are.[1Co.12:27] But this traditional concept can minimize, or even impoverish the *personal vitality* of the living presence of Christ *within* the believer.

Many Christians leave the ministry of witnessing to others whom they consider to be more qualified or more spiritual than they are. They say, "The church, the Sunday School, the ladies' society, the men's group, the youth teams — *they* are qualified to do the witnessing." These kinds of believers want their church to be involved in sharing Christ's message with the unconverted, and they are willing to pay the expenses for the good news to be shared, but they feel that *others are more qualified than they are to do the job.*

Christianity is a *personal* thing. If Christ has come to dwell in us, we are His body. He wills to be interpreted through us. It is through our lives and our personalities that He wants to be represented in our communities. The essence of our Christian experience is *Christ* [living, working, ministering] *in us*.Col.1:27

When Jesus was in Nazareth, *He could do no mighty work there...because of unbelief*.Mk.6:5-6 Without human faith on the part of people in Nazareth, Christ's ministry was limited then. Without faith that He is at work *in and through us today*, His ministry is still limited.

Unique Privilege

Many people imagine or think that God will eventually send angels to proclaim this gospel to the world. Very often Christians pray and wait for God to do what He told them to do. The Bible says that *the glorious gospel...has been **committed to our trust**.*1Ti.1:11; 1Th.2:4; 1Co.9:17; Gal.2:7 He ordained that ordinary people like you and like me are to communicate the good news to *every creature*, in *all the world*. If we do not do it, the message of Christ and His love will not be communicated.

Paul said, *I thank Christ Jesus our Lord, who hath **enabled** me for that he counted me faithful, putting me into the ministry*.1Ti.1:11-12 The gospel is now *committed* to us. He has now *enabled* us. He now *counts us faithful.* The witness of Christ now depends on us.

Christ wants to visit the incarcerated of our community, but He needs human persons to function through. When *we* visit those in prison, then *He* visits them.

This is biblical Christianity! Everything else is ritualistic, ceremonial. Christ lives *in* us. That gives purpose to our lives. We have been filled with His Spirit for a reason—not just to warm a church pew and to be "spiritual," but *to go beyond the walls of our church sanctuary to tell others about Jesus Christ and His love.*

Christ In Action
Through Christian Believers

Many times Christians pray and tell God all the things that they want Him to do. Their prayers sound very humble as they send Him all of their orders for the day or the week.

Much prayer time is wasted by people asking God for two things that He will never do: 1) They ask Him to do *what He has already done.* 2) They ask Him to do *what He has told them to do.*

The Holy Spirit is not a heavenly agent that we can dispatch to accomplish *our* missions in life. He functions *through us* as believers. *We* are His temple today.[1Co.3:16-17,6:19] He moves among people when *we* do. He accomplishes His mission *in* us and *through* us.

His Mission—Our Mission

Here is a most significant Bible verse to remember in this regard. While I was preaching to thousands of people in the Ukraine, I quoted this verse: *When Christ had by himself purged our sins, he sat down on the right hand of the Majesty on high.*[Heb.1:3] It was like a huge banner was unfurled across the skies before me bearing these words:

"Of Course He Sat Down; There Was Nothing More For Him To Do. He Had Committed Gospel Ministry To Us"

Christ accomplished our redemption so perfectly that He was able to fully empower us to continue the ministry that He began. Through His vicarious death, burial and resurrection, He restored us to God as His friends and co-workers. The commission to carry the gospel to all nations was *entrusted to us*, along with His Holy Spirit Who endowed us with His same power and virtue.

His work of redemption was so complete that we were *brought back into the very presence of God, and are standing there before Him with nothing left against us.*[Col.1:22LB] Since Christ gave His life to reconcile us to God, He could then come and live *in* us because our sins no longer *separated between* us and our God and no longer hid His face from us.[Isa.59:2]

In the gospels, Christ gave us His example in ministry. He showed us the Father's will. Then in redemption, He transferred to us His nature, His anointing, His power, His name, His righteousness, His glory, His authority. With that divine endowment, He entrusted to us His commission to take His message to our hurting world.

After *purging us from our* sins, making us worthy to share His life and virtue, **He sat down.** But it is not our time to sit down. It is our time to **stand up!** His redemptive work is *finished.* Now He has committed to us the continuation of His ministry, as His representatives, as His interpreters. He has now delegated us to *go* with the good news, as His ambassadors, and to act on His behalf and in His name.

God reconciled us to himself through Christ and has [now] given us the ministry of reconciliation…. We are therefore Christ's ambassadors…[2Co.5:18NIV] After He ascended back to the Father, He became our mediator,[1Ti.2:5] and we became His representatives to continue His ministry.

Jesus said, *You have not chosen me but I have chosen you, and ordained you, that you should go and bring forth fruit, and that your fruit should remain: that whatever you shall ask of the Father in my name, he may give it you.*[Jn.15:16]

33

Endowed by Christ with His name, His word and His Holy Spirit, we now act on His behalf, in His name and for His glory—not imploring Him to do the things that He sent us to do. Today Christ ministers *through* **us** *as His authorized ambassadors.*

The Human Channel

The Church of Christ is not a building. It is the converted people. We are His voice today. Now He walks in our shoes. He touches with our hands. He listens with our ears and embraces with our arms of love.

The Church cannot send Christ or His Holy Spirit out as a spiritual messenger to bless the poor, to comfort the distressed, to visit the sick and to persuade those who are lost to believe the gospel. The only way He can visit the sick and witness to *un*saved people is through believers like you and me. He now touches people through our hands and embraces them with our arms. He hears people through our ears and perceives their needs through our eyes. He now speaks to people through our lips

Christ's ministry in any community is limited to those through whom He is allowed to live and express Himself. He longs to speak to people about salvation, to convince them of the gospel, but He can only do it through believers who allow Him to speak through their lips.

If Christians are too busy to go and witness or to share their Lord's message, then He has no other channel to minister through, and the unconverted world may be lost. Those who are sick and in prison may never be visited by Christ if believers do not go as His representatives and minister to them in His name. *People may never see God if they do not see Him in action through Christian believers like you and me.*

That is why it is vital that we express our witness of Christ *outside the walls of the church sanctuary.* That is where hurting and despairing people are to be found. Sharing Christ's love with them is the most vital and spiritual ministry possible for followers of our Lord today.

Redemption Reality

Bible teachers emphasize that the Holy Spirit was *with* the followers of Christ before the day of Pentecost, but they stress that He is *in* believers now.[Jn.14:17]

That is where He is—*in* those of us who have received Him. He is not floating around the world, carrying out orders for believers, hovering over human beings, solving their problems and blessing people, while Christians live tranquil, personal lives in privacy.

Christ visits the needy and uplifts the fallen through believers. He encourages the discouraged and gives hope to the despondent through human persons in whom He lives. He heals the brokenhearted and binds up the wounds of the suffering through ordinary people like you and me.

That is why that, although prayer is vital in the lives of believers, if we fail to do more than just pray for the unconverted—if we do not visit the lost and witness to the unsaved, then those people may never hear Christ's invitation to be saved.

Our Regal Mission

We are Christ's interpreters and associates, authorized to represent Him in our world. *Now then we are ambassadors for Christ.*[2Co.5:20] That means that we are empowered to act on His behalf and in His name. We are to carry out His policies for people. We are not the ones to plan God's day for Him. He plans our day for us. It is His embassy that we are serving in. He is not serving in ours. He is not our messenger. *We are His.*

It is not our place to give orders and to map errands for the Holy Spirit to carry out on our behalf. *He has given the orders for us to carry out on His behalf.* If we are too busy with our private business or other personal interests to be concerned

36

with people who will not enter church sanctuaries to learn about God, then they may never receive a biblical witness of Christ or experience His divine *gift of Love*.

The Holy Spirit acts and ministers *through us*, communicating and revealing Jesus to our world.[Jn.15:26,16:14-15] If we are too busy to witness for Him, He has no other channel for action. He lives in us. Now we are His Temple. *OR ARE we A PRISON OR TOMB?*

Christians do not intentionally imprison Christ within their houses or their church sanctuaries — or within themselves. But unless they allow Him to speak to people and to share His good news through them, He is restrained from being able to communicate His love to people in our hurting world. He said, *The Son of man is come to seek and to save that which was lost.*[Lu.19:10] Paul said. *This is a faithful saying, and worthy of all acceptation, that Christ Jesus came into the world to save sinners.*[1Ti.1:15]

Christ Helping People—Through YOU

Have you shared with someone the way of salvation and offered to help them to receive Christ's life? Has He been able to speak good news through your lips? Have you permitted Him to look through your eyes into the face of someone who is hurting and to speak words of comfort? Have you permitted Him to touch someone who is lonely or frightened or in despair, through your hands? Or to embrace some-one who needs help, using your arms? Or to lend strength to someone who is faltering, by using your shoulder for them to lean on?

This is biblical Christianity — *Christ living today in and through ordinary human persons like you and like me.*

Are you concerned about the lives of uncon-verted people in your neighborhood and else-where? Have you informed some of them or shared the uplifting lifestyle of Jesus Christ?

Have you assumed that such matters are the re-sponsibility of the *Church*? You are correct. But the Church is not the congregation nor the de-nomination. *The Church is you and it is me.* Christ has endowed us with that supreme honor.

The Lord does not live in a stone cathedral or in a temple of bricks and mortar. He lives in our lives — in our bodies. We are His temple. He min-isters, exhibits Himself, demonstrates His com-passion and extends His mercy through people like you and like me, and through others like us. This is our divine heritage that makes our Chris-tian lives worth living.

*This truth is **the heartbeat of soulwinning**.* Eve-rything else is ceremonial. We can automate the rituals of the Christian religion. *But the dynamics of the Christ-Life must be an inspiration, a revela-tion — a miracle in our lives.*

When the Lord spoke to Philip telling him to *join this chariot,*[Ac.8:29] He was saying to us too: "Go out to the busy thoroughfares of life, out where the world is on the move, and find those who are lost; witness to them of Christ, inform them of His good news, and share His love with them."

As believers go beyond their sanctuary walls, — out where the people are, out among the traffic and din of humanity, out in public places and in private homes, *there is where the Holy Spirit will guide them into encounters where they can lead needy and lonely human persons to faith in Jesus Christ*, just as Philip led the eunuch to Him.[Ac.8:26-38]

This is the ministry that is open to every Christian, regardless of age, race, gender, culture, or social background.

✧ ✧ ✧

WE SHALL NOW look at some of the marvelous spiritual developments in churches and among Christian believers today where the First Century passion for souls has been rekindled.

Chapter 5

A Time For Reflection

THE EARLY CHURCH had no better salvation than believing followers of Christ have today.

The baptism of the Holy Spirit was no more real in Bible days than it is in the lives of committed Christians today.

The righteousness of Christ was no more valid then, than it is in the lives of believers today.

Sanctification was no more effective then than it is now. The gifts of the Spirit were no more authentic then than today.

The knowledge that early Christians had of the message of salvation and their ministry to the sick and suffering was no more trustworthy in the First Century than it is among believers in this 21st Century.

Those First Century Christians understood the purpose for which they have received the Holy Spirit in their lives. Many Christians today have not made that discovery.

The majority of church members in this epoch have not ventured beyond their sanctuary walls to witness for Christ. Most of them pray that *un-converted* people will be saved, and they may invite some of them to their church, but they have little social contact with the *non*-Christian world.

By contrast, the Early Church was engaged in a continuous house to house, market to market, person to person witnessing ministry. The *uncon-verted* world needs the friendship and fellowship of Christian believers who are concerned about their problems, pains, dilemmas and insecurities.

Spirituality Craze

There is a woman who claims the gift of casting out devils by speaking in tongues. While sitting in the congregation, she is seized by this *power*, stands up in a frenzy and speaks in *tongues* to drive out the evil spirits from the *Christians* who are present. She does not claim to know who is possessed of these spirits, but she believes that her barrage of tongues *exorcises* them from who-ever may be possessed.

Many good people have become so absorbed in their desire for spiritual *depth* that they have for-gotten that the true ministry of believers is to witness of Christ and to win people to Him. Without the objective of witnessing to the lost, Christians can become so distorted and confused

41

in their phobic pursuit of *spirituality* that fanaticism and extremism can result. An example is the wide-spread *glossolalia* rage which has almost become a religious ritual.

If the only evidence that I had been baptized in the Holy Spirit had been speaking in other tongues, I would not be satisfied. Too many people have jubilated in *glossololia* who obviously never received the supernatural witnessing power that First Century Christians received. Jesus said, *You shall receive **power** after that the Holy Ghost is come upon you: and **you shall be witnesses unto me**...unto the uttermost part of the earth.*[Ac.1:8] This apostolic, biblical *dunamis* merits careful reappraisal in view of extremisms among certain religious consortiums today.

Communicating Christ

During more than a half century of ministry as a team, Daisy and I proclaimed the gospel together to millions of people of most major religious backgrounds in seventy-three nations. We have concluded that the masses of *un*converted people in our world do not need to hear people who speak in *"other"* tongues. They need desperately to hear people who communicate the message of Christ in the tongues that these masses can understand.

While so many Christians are banqueting at exhibitions of spiritual gifts and ecstatic manifestations, a significant rediscovery of personal soulwinning has been taking place among tens of thousands of believers around the world who care about the *un*converted world.

There is a renewed awareness of the spiritual power and gifts that relate to the ministry of winning lost souls to Christ. This is the purpose of the baptism of the Holy Spirit — *to empower gospel believers to witness convincingly that Jesus is the Christ, the Son of God, the Savior of the world, risen from the dead and is the author and mediator of redemption.*

Until late in the 20th Century, almost all Christians (except those of the Early Church) have remained church-bound, content to sit in their sanctuaries and to be *holy*. But that attitude has now become *démodé* as believers return to the busy crossroads and to the dwellings of the *un*converted, *taking Christ to them* instead of waiting for them to *come to the church*. This return to biblical Christianity is resulting in multiplied millions of people coming to Christ worldwide.

◇ ◇ ◇

A FEW YEARS ago a Christian leader was teaching a church Bible class as a visiting guest.

He asked, "How many of you here are Christians?"

Everyone raised their hands, and the regular teacher exulted, "Wonderful!"

But the guest teacher countered, "No, this is not wonderful. We should have *un*believers here in this class being influenced to Christ by the truths that are being taught here."

Many church buildings are almost completely segregated from the *unconverted* world. The sanctuary has been called *"the sacred spot where little groups of sanctimonious people meet and minister to themselves in pious seclusion."*

But that attitude has drastically changed in recent years. Christians are rediscovering the passion for souls that motivated First Century believers to share Christ's message with the hurting, *un*converted people of their world.

✧ ✧ ✧

AN EVANGELIST TRIED to arouse a small Japanese congregation to be more evangelistic. The local pastor objected, "You don't understand. We don't want a large crowd. We want a small group of faithful believers who can meet together in quietness to study God's Word and learn of Him in depth."

44

A philosophy like that has become *passé* as believers have learned to recognize that they are Christ's hands, arms, feet, legs and heart today — that the only way He can minister to *un*converted people is through Christians in whom He dwells.

◇ ◇ ◇

ANOTHER SOULWINNER encouraged a men's prayer group to begin a program of witnessing for Christ from house to house. The leader responded: "We can't do that. We're not spiritually deep enough in God."

"How long have you been meeting and praying?" asked the evangelist.

"Only two years," the group leader replied.

For two years those Christian men had been meeting and studying God's word, but they had never discovered the joy of allowing the Lord to minister *through them* to the hurting people of their community.

In the Book of Acts, within a similar period of just *two years*, those early Christians made the word of the Lord known to **all who dwelt in Asia**.^{Ac.19:10}

It is encouraging to see that Christians today are discovering that spiritual *depth* is not drowning ones self in some doctrinal ecstasy; it is in giving of ones self to share Christ with others.

The reason the gospel has not been preached *to every creature* is because Christians have misunderstood *what*, or *who* the Church really is. It is biblical to refer to the church as the collective body of Christ.[Ro.12:5; 1Co.12:12,27] But from an individual standpoint, you and I must grasp the fact that the church is *you* — it is *me*. When we accepted Jesus Christ as our Lord and Savior, our body became His body. *It is the temple of the Holy Ghost.*[1Co.6:19]

Jesus was a soulwinner. He mixed with people. He befriended the needy, healed the sick and communicated good news to people. He has never changed. He wills to do the same today — through people like you and me. Paul says that He works in us *both desiring and doing his good pleasure.*[Ph.2:13]

Jesus Christ ministers to needy people today *through believers,* as they allow Him free expression through their lives, their emotions, their attitudes. He can minister to people only as Christians allow Him to minister *through* them.

◇ ◇ ◇

THERE WAS A man who had directed the evangelism department of a large church for thirty-three years. During that period, the congregation had realized no increase. The church elected a new pastor who was a zealous soulwinner. As soon as he was installed, he invited their director of evangelism to join him for a day of door to door witnessing.

When they returned that night, several souls had been led to accept Christ. The evangelism director fell on his knees in the young pastor's office and confessed in tears: "I've been responsible for our church's evangelism ministry for all of these years without ever seeing a soul saved. Today I have gained a knowledge of my Lord that I have never experienced before."

He had helped lead *un*converted people to Jesus Christ out in their own homes.

✧ ✧ ✧

A LADY WHO was a faithful member of a church became involved in an affair with a married man. When the episode was discovered, she was ashamed and left the church, resolving never to return.

The women in the church held a special meeting to pray for their sister. But they did more. They delegated two of their number to go find the woman and to express their love and concern for her. That was the Spirit of Christ, the Good Shepherd, at work in those ladies.^{Mt.18:11-12}

Throughout the day they sought for their embarrassed sister without success. The next day, they resumed their search and found her in a dingy apartment, alone and depressed.

"Come back to church," they urged.

"I could never do that," the dispirited woman replied. "I've caused too much shame."

"But we *want* you to come back. We need you."

"Do the women *want* me? Do they need *me?*"

"Yes, they sent us to tell you that we love you. We need you. Come back home."

The lady returned to those who loved her. She was forgiven, encouraged in the love of Christ, and resumed her place in the work of God.

This happened because some Christian women allowed Jesus, the Good Shepherd, to *leave the ninety and nine, and go...seek that which was gone astray. And finding it, there was more rejoicing over that sheep, than over [all the others] which went not astray.* Mt.18:12-13

Look, Listen, Reach

At first, you may be afraid or timid or hesitant to act in Christ's stead, but do it! Reach out to someone, remembering that you are acting in His name. He and you are partners. You are His ambassador or ambassadress. He is *with* you and He is *in* you. Yield your emotions to Him so that they can reflect His attitude. He will help you to discover a dimension of Himself and of His lifestyle, expressed *in* and *through* you, that you never experienced before.

This commitment does not put a *halo* above your head. It is simply an awareness that a real Christian believer is someone who cares about people, who looks into people's eyes, who is sensitive to human needs, who is willing to touch a shoulder or a hand with comfort and encouragement, or just to lend an ear to listen.

People need God. People need people. People find God by finding people who care about people. Christians are sharers of their faith, of their hope, of their love and of their Christ, and the Holy Spirit will always guide you and manifest God's love *through* you. *The love of God is shed abroad in our hearts by the Holy Ghost.* Ro.5:5

Some ask, "How can I know when or how God is speaking to me and leading me to do something?"

My answer: *Listen*, and you will hear. *Look*, and you will see. *Reach* out and you will touch. You will know God's voice. Always remember this simple rule: if your idea is *good for God*, if it is *good for people*, and if it is *good for you*, then you can be sure the idea is from God, that it is His voice that you are hearing.

So put those ideas into action—the ones that will help and lift somebody and that will bring glory to God. Who else but the Spirit of our Lord would impress you to go and share Christ with someone in need?

◇ ◇ ◇

AFTER ATTENDING CHURCH one night, a certain Christian could not go to sleep. He felt impressed to talk to a man about Christ's love.

Finally, after midnight, he arose, dressed himself, and went to his friend's house. When he knocked, the man came to the door at once.

The Christian apologized: "I know that it looks foolish for me to be knocking on your door at such an hour."

"Not at all," came the quick reply. "I've had no rest. I've felt that I must get right with God and I need help. You are the very person that I wanted to talk with because I have confidence in your life." And the man received Christ as his savior that night.

You will grow deepest in God by sharing Him with others who need His love. He will become more real to you than ever before, as you allow Him to minister *through your life*—through *YOU*. You are His church, His temple, His body.

This is the cardinal truth that is the *heartbeat of biblical Christianity* – sharing the gospel and the love of Christ with hurting people.

Visitation or Soulwinning

It is important that we distinguish between a pious, formal, organized *visitation program*, and an enthusiastic, personal commitment to seize each opportunity to share Christ and His love.

The Church has recovered the fundamental doctrines of First Century Christianity. But it has taken a long time for the ministry of *personal witnessing among the unconverted* to regain the place it occupied in the Early Church. An international revival of this truth is under way. There is evidence that it is finding renewed prominence in Christian ministries around the world, particularly in emerging nations.

It is often assumed that ordinary church members are not qualified to lead souls to Christ. They are usually told to bring unsaved people to the church where the pastor, who is qualified in such matters, can deal with them about salvation.

✧ ✧ ✧

A YOUNG CHRISTIAN in England attended one of our soulwinning seminars. She was so inspired by what we shared that she went out and began witnessing among non-conformist youth groups, and within a few days, she had won several of them to Christ.

She asked a pastor if she might bring her new converts to the church, and he was elated. But she failed to explain that their appearance might not conform to traditional standards.

When she arrived with her troupe of new converts, it was a shock to the pious pastor. He immediately called the young soulwinner aside and reprimanded her for having brought such people into their sanctuary. She was told not to bring them again until their hair and dress styles were *appropriate*.

The pastor informed the young soulwinner: "Your place is in church where you can learn to be a proper Christian. You have no business making a public mockery of the house of God by bringing such people into the House of God. You leave the work of evangelism to those of us who are qualified for such things."

But this young Christian had done exactly what the early followers of Christ did. After the woman of Samaria believed on Him, she *left her waterpot, and went her way into the city and said...Come, see a man, which told me all things that ever I did: is not this the Christ? Then they went out of the city, and came to him.*Jn.4:28-30 *And many of the Samaritans of that city believed on him for the saying* *of the woman...and many more believed because of his own word.*[Jn.4:39,41]

The world does not want religion proffered by pious pontificates. People want to know about Jesus Christ in simple terms that they can comprehend.

The most rewarding experience for a believer is to encounter someone who is *un*saved, out in their own *milieu*, and help them to embrace Christ.

Changes In Recent Decades

For generations, Christians have generally hibernated within their sanctuary walls, out of touch with the *un*converted world. These negative attitudes have fostered the impression that believers have little interest in those who are *un*converted.

Many traditional church members seemed to be saying by their action: "*Un*converted people know that we are here. If they want to be saved, let them come to our church. Here, we can help them to find Christ. We love them. We conduct special evangelism services to preach to them. We pray for them. We have our choir, our personal workers, our preacher, our mourner's bench. Here we are equipped to help them find Christ— *if they will come to our church.*"

But Christians who embrace such ideas have forgotten that the appeal of a church building or a denomination to hurting people is exactly *zero*. Yet the exciting fact persists that the greatest appeal possible to the human heart, is *the person of Jesus Christ.*

How *Not* To Succeed

Suppose a business company sent out public invitations: "The *General Product Company* invites you and your family to attend our special market meeting. We have an excellent program. The choir from our sales college will sing, and our sales manager who is an great orator will speak. Come and be inspired by this event."

Their strategy: To attract potential customers to buy their products.

The company would soon be bankrupt—not because their products were inferior, but because their sales would be limited to the few who would get dressed, drive across town, listen to a sales talk, and purchase something.

This could be an example of what Jesus meant when He said: *The children of this world are in their generation wiser that the children of light.*[Lu.16:8]

Hurting People
Waiting For A Touch

The owner of a large hotel in Holland was converted in our historic crusade in The Hague. Over 100,000 people attended each meeting. For days after his conversion, that man was heard going from table to table in his hotel dining room, witnessing to his guests and urging them to believe on Christ.

A new convert wants others to receive the Lord. The world of *un*converted people wants to know about Jesus Christ. They are weary of religious rituals and are waiting for the voice and the touch of someone who has experienced salvation and who is so grateful for what Christ has done that they cannot keep silent about Him.

Successful churches conduct training classes to prepare members for teaching. In the same way, systematic soulwinning classes can inspire and motivate believers for personal evangelism. The Bible says, *the one who wins souls is wise.*[Pr.11:30]

Companies train sales people. Sect leaders train adherents. Churches train teachers. After years of church programs to attract people to the sanctuary, we are witnessing significant changes. The Church is training believers in the art of winning souls. Bible schools and seminaries have begun to offer courses on personal witnesses. Many of them are using this book as their text book. The new focus, today among alert churches is _outside_ _the sanctuary_. That is the golden key to the success of First Century believers.

Soulwinning Regains Prominence

As personal evangelism regains prominence today, the Bible is becoming a fresh, new guide for tens of thousands of believers. Astute writers are producing papers, bulletins, reviews, journals, expositions, magazines, books, manuals and other publications on the vital subject of _Soulwinning_. Many effective courses have been designed, published and are being taught in evangelism programs today. Teachers who are experienced in soulwinning are in demand around the world.

Pastors are discovering fresh inspiration for teaching about winning the lost to Christ as the early believers did. Evangelists are teaching believers to witness for Christ, as part of their ministries. Youth groups are finding new methods of ministry and new purpose for living. Believers, both men and women, are discovering new dimensions of _serving God by serving people_. Dormant congregations are coming to life. An era of renewed Christianity is commanding the stage of action again.

✧ ✧ ✧

TODAY, BELIEVERS face the most unique and formidable epoch of all of Christian history. Never before have so many *un*evangelized millions been *reachable* with the gospel. And never before have Christians had access to so much *information* and to such potentially *effective means and methods* for winning millions to Christ.

We shall look next at a traditional concept that has influenced believers to remain *quarantined* within their worship centers, hindering them from taking the good news out to the people — on their own terrain.

Chapter 6

The Notorious Mental Block

WHAT IS THE DIFFERENCE between *Revival* and *Evangelism*? Or have you thought about it? Or does it matter?

Revival is *re*viving something that had life before. You cannot *re*vive what never lived. But *Evangelism* is giving new life to those who are *dead in trespasses and sins,*[Ep.2:1] — who have never experienced God's *Life* before.

Revival is for Christians. Evangelism is for *non*-Christians – for the *un*believing world.

Christians received life from Christ when they believed the gospel and accepted Him as their savior. But since they may become *lukewarm* [Re.3:16] or may have *left their first love,*[Re.2:4] they may need *re*vival.

Inside the church building is the place for revival. Outside the church building is the place for evangelism.

This book concerns evangelism. That is why we call it *Soulwinning*. This apostolic ministry has been greatly impeded by a notorious mental block that assumes that if *un*saved people can be persuaded to come to the church building, then they can be influenced to embrace Christ and be saved.

So a special speaker is brought to the church. Advertisements appeal to the public to come to hear their invited guest. Announcements are publicized by radio, television, e-mail, the internet and by newspaper. But very few *un*saved people respond.

Why? Because *non*-Christians are not interested in going into church buildings.

Outdated Mentality

But the out-of-date Christian mind-set ignores this fact. Church members love their sanctuary, their freshly carpeted aisles and newly padded pews. Their choir is well-trained and they are proud of their pastor. They believe that with enough advertisement, the *un*converted will be persuaded to come to their church.

Singers, musicians, performers, and special choirs are engaged. The faithful ones spread the news and the welcome mat is rolled out. House to house calls are made, inviting people to hear the entertainers at the church. Advertisement is intensified, but the results are still mediocre. A handful of church absentees and some dropouts attend and may be revived. But few *non*-Christians attend the events.

Thousands were invited. Why did not more of them respond? Because *un*saved people are not interested in coming to church.

Someone may argue, "That's a pessimistic view. We don't share that conclusion. We'll find something that will attract *un*converted people to our church."

So more musicians or singers or performers or speakers are scheduled. More advertisements and more promotion are scheduled. Believers are urged to more earnest prayer. Again the church doors swing open and the welcome mat is rolled out. And a precious few are persuaded to attend the meetings. Some are even converted and those few who do get saved are worth the effort because a single soul won to Christ is worth whatever investment is made to reach them.

But, in general, very few *un*converted people respond. The groundwork is well laid. The believers spare nothing, but the efforts made do not bear much fruit. Faithful Christians ask in dismay: "Why?"

The Persistent Answer

The *unconverted* world has been trying to tell Christians something for a long time: "Your pastor may have a Ph.D., you may air-condition your building, carpet your aisles, cushion your pews, invite us to your church via radio, television, phone calls, letters, church bulletins, newspaper ads, electronic mail, or personal visits; you may bring preachers, lecturers, prophets, teachers, evangelists, musicians, entertainers, or singers, *but we are not interested in coming to your church!*"

So churches that have not updated their philosophy ask in consternation, "What must we do to attract *unconverted* people to our meetings so they can be saved?" The answer is simple: *Abandon the traditional mental block.*

Where The Need Is Obvious

If the testimony of Christ is only shared within the walls of the sanctuary, then the majority of *unconverted* people will never discover Christ in their lives because they will not be present.

There are millions of needy, despairing, lonely, fearful, *unloved* and neglected people who would be responsive and receptive to Christ if someone witnessed to them. They are waiting—right out there beyond the sanctuary. They need salvation, they want forgiveness, they search for knowledge about God, they fear to die as they are, they are encompassed with problems and they yearn for help, but most of them will never come to church.

When Christian believers go to them and give them the gospel, *out where they live and work and play*, they accept Christ and receive His salvation.

Then with confidence in those believers who shared Christ's love with them, they gladly follow them back to their churches where they grow in grace and in the knowledge of Christ. They know that someone cared for them, came to them and helped them to receive Christ on their own terrain.

Two Words That Count

The most timid Christian who witnesses of Christ to an *un*converted person says two of the most powerful words in our language before he or she ever opens their mouth: They say, *"I care!"* People want to be loved; they want to know that someone cares for them.

There is a church whose members win more people to Christ than any other one in its denomination. The pastor was asked : "Do you win people by attracting them to your Sunday School classes or to special evangelistic meetings at your church?"

His reply: "No, we win almost no one that way. We live in an area of strong religious loyalties. Almost no one will visit our church. So we go to the people's homes and workplaces to share Christ with them and that's where we win them. Then they come to our church and become strong believers."

First—To Christ; Then—To Church

Most churches teach their members how to invite people to their *sanctuary*. First Century believers focused on inviting people to *Christ*. New Testament Christians testified and taught people *publicly and from house to house,*[Ac.20:20] making disciples out where the people lived and worked and played.

Their focus was to win people to Christ, *then* to welcome them to their meeting places. That concept succeeds today the same as it did in the Early Church. Evangelism is the grand theme of biblical ministry—to *preach the gospel to every creature.*[Mk.16:15]

✧ ✧ ✧

AS CHRISTIANS SHARE Christ with *unconverted* people—on their own territory like First Century believers did, they rediscover the most rewarding ministry that Christ ever committed to His followers—*being His witnesses.*[Ac.1:8]

There was a balance in the Early Church that we shall look at in the next chapter. It formed the foundation for their tremendous success in spreading the gospel across their world.

Chapter 7

The "*20-20*" Vision

*A*ND DAILY IN *the temple and in every house,* *they ceased not to teach and preach Jesus Christ.*^{Ac.5:42}

They did it *in the temples.* They did it *in every house.* They did it *daily.* They *did not cease* doing it.^{Ac.2:46}

What resulted from their action? *The Lord added to the church daily such as should be saved.*^{Acts 2:47}

The Lord can only add to the Church *daily* if Christian believers witness to *un*believers *daily.* My sister, Nellie Roberts, ministered daily as an involved and compassionate soulwinner in her community of Katy, Texas, almost until her demise at the age of 93. She was headlined in her town newspaper as *Katy's Angel.* Why? Because she was busy every day, teaching in the neighborhood, visiting the sick and shut-ins, comforting lonely persons, praying for those who were suffering, encouraging those in despair – and always witnessing about Jesus Christ and His love.

I had another sister, Pastor Daisy Gillock. She and her husband, both deceased now, pioneered three Assemblies of God churches in West Texas. The focus of their ministry was to go out among the *unconverted*, witnessing of Christ and leading people to Him wherever they could be encountered. Their lives were committed to sharing Christ with those who did not know the love of God.

If Christians witness *daily — in their place of worship and in every house,* the Lord can add to their number *daily.* That means that their number can increase by at least three hundred and sixty-five converts each year.

Productive Agenda

The Bible says, *And the word of God increased.*^{Ac.6:7} Another verse says, *and the Lord added to the church daily such as should be saved.*^{Ac.2:47} Then it says, *the number of the disciples multiplied greatly.*^{Ac.6:7} Those early Christians were successful, and the same results are being realized today when believers recapture that *First Century passion for souls.*

The Balanced Vision

Paul said, *I kept back nothing that was profitable to you and have taught you* 1] *publicly and* 2] *from house to house.*^{Ac.20:20}

It is a numerical coincidence that Acts chapter twenty, verse twenty, indicates the balanced *twenty-twenty* vision of First Century Christians. They preached the gospel and witnessed of Christ *publicly* and also from *house to house*. They practiced those ministries *daily*.

There is another verse in the Book of Acts that says, *this continued for a period of twenty [!] years, so that all those who lived in Asia heard the word of the Lord Jesus, both Jews and Greeks.*[Ac.19:10]

Just *twenty* years? And **all** *those who lived in Asia* received a gospel witness.

Did you notice that I misquoted the record? It does not say twenty years. It says **two** years. *By the space of two years, all they which dwelt in Asia heard the word of the Lord.*

Conquest Without Convenience

They had no ocean vessels, automobiles, airplanes or even bicycles; they had no electricity, public-address systems or loud speakers; no newspapers, printing presses, radios, televisions or other public media; no audio or video cassette players, dictating machines, electronic mail or computers; not even typewriters, fountain pens, or lead and ball-point pencils.

How did those First Century believers accomplish so much, within such a short time? They considered themselves to be Christ's witnesses. They **ceased not** *to teach and preach Jesus Christ.*Ac.5:42 That was their passion. They were *believers.* What Christ has accomplished in their lives was so remarkably real that they could not restrain themselves from sharing the good news with others.

They witnessed *daily in the temple and in every house.* This was done, not by the apostles, but by the believers. The record says, *there was a great persecution against the church...and they were **all** scattered abroad...**except the apostles**...and they that were scattered abroad went every where **preaching the word**.*Ac.8:1,4

◇ ◇ ◇

ALL OF THOSE Early Church believers, both men and women, were preachers, witnesses, talkers, communicators, reporters, and transmitters of Christ's message. They were in action on behalf of their Lord and Savior, *out where the people were.*

That compassion for the *unconverted* has, in recent decades, reinvigorated concerned pastors, Christian leaders and churches around the world.

In our next chapter, we will share some examples of the amazing results that are being experienced where believers are being motivated to witness for Christ *out where the people are.* This focus is inspiring stalemated church members to initiate successful soulwinning ministries.

Chapter 8

An Inspired Approach

"**W**E'RE GOING TO begin an Evangelistic Crusade," the young pastor announced to his small congregation. "During this soulwinning event, our church will be closed—except on Sundays."

What did he mean? How could a local church carry on an evangelistic crusade with the doors of the sanctuary closed?

Ever since the Dark Ages, traditional church ministry patterns have been just the opposite: The church sanctuary has been the center of action.

But if evangelism is limited to the sanctuary, the young pastor insisted, they could not reach the *un*converted. He was only twenty-four years old and had just finished Bible school. Looking for a suitable location for his first pastorate, he located an old church building that had been closed. Boards had been nailed over the doors and windows.

New Life In An Old House

At one time, the old church had over eight hundred members, being located in the elite section of the city. But now, the wealthy people had moved away and poor people had occupied the neighborhood.

The young preacher located the remaining members of the board and prevailed upon them to elect him as their pastor and to permit him to re-open the old church.

Then he went to an orphanage and won approval for forty orphans to attend the opening church meeting on Sunday. So he began with those orphans, with seven members of the old church board and with his own family. The young pastor was passionate about winning souls so that was the focus of his teaching.

Then he made his brave announcement: "We're going to begin an Evangelistic Crusade. During this soulwinning event, our church will be closed — except on Sundays."

Each evening that handful of Christian believers met for prayer. Each was assigned a different street, and they began their biblical evangelism crusade, knocking on doors, witnessing to people about Christ and His love. On weekends, they regrouped at the old church building for prayer and inspiration.

Four Sundays later, they had an attendance of two hundred and twenty people, and the spirit of their evangelism crusade had affected each of their converts.

They Caught The Vision

With no outside evangelist, no extra church expenses, no added heat or air conditioning bills to pay, that church reaped a harvest of souls. They caught the vision of biblical soulwinning—*out among the unconverted*. They had a new passion for souls and made the grand discovery that *un*converted people are easy to win—if you share Christ with them out where they are.

The pastor said later: "Now we have only one problem; our people only want to win souls." At the end of the year, that church had won more people to Christ than any other church in the city.

❖ ❖ ❖

A NEW SOULWINNING church was celebrating its fifth anniversary. In one year it had reached a membership of forty-four people. Now its attendance was over two thousand.

At the end of their first year they were still meeting in a garage. Their property was only worth about six thousand dollars, and their annual budget was about the same. But at the end of their fifth year, their annual budget was two hundred thousand dollars and their property was valued at more than a million dollars. In their five year history, they had outgrown five buildings. How did they accomplish that?

The pastor had trained about ten of his people and they had gone from door to door, witnessing to *un*converted people, winning them to Christ.

The first year, they won a hundred and fifty souls—most of them inside their own homes. The next year over three hundred new converts had been brought into the church. The third year, they had won over five hundred people. During their fifth year, more then seven hundred people had been saved.

The pastor said: "Today we have more ushers passing offering plates than we had members four years ago." They were sponsoring forty-four people on mission fields—which was the number of members they had four years earlier.

When an evangelist questioned them about their success, the pastor said, "Come to our mid-week service and you will see for yourself."

At their Wednesday meeting, more than seven hundred believers were present. The pastor asked the congregation, "How many of you have gone outside our sanctuary this year and have won at least one soul to Christ?" Over three hundred people stood to their feet.

That church had rediscovered the soulwinning secret of First Century believers. They had proven that if Christians care about *un*converted people and want to lead them to Christ, any believer can do it by going and witnessing of Christ, *out where the unsaved people live and work and play.*

✧ ✧ ✧

A CERTAIN PASTOR has the distinction of baptizing more new converts each year than other widely known ministers. His church is among the most successful in the world. An evangelist asked him, "Why is it that your church brings more newly converted people into its fellowship than almost any other church?"

He answered with four words: "Our people win souls." Those words reveal the secret to biblical evangelism. Then he explained: "We have emphasized one truth among our people until they have come to believe it."

Then he stated this Bible verse: *Daily in the temple and in every house, they ceased not to teach and preach Jesus Christ.*Ac.5:42

Someone from that church visits in the home of every family that moves into their city. They contact as many as ten thousand people in one week.

The pastor says that he consistently teaches Christian witnessing and the people believe that their personal ministry is to win souls. The pastor himself sets the example. Sharing Christ's love with the *un*converted is the one magnificent obsession of the members of that church.

❖ ❖ ❖

YOU MIGHT THINK that these churches are too large to be examples for your church in your area.

*Un*converted people live in communities of all sizes. People of any area, social standing, ethnic background or economic level are responsive to the message of Christ if they are reached with the gospel — *out where they live and work and play.*

The pastor of a small rural community church said, "I can stand on our church roof and see only two houses."

When he became the pastor in that community, attendance was about seventy-five people. The entire area population was around four hundred.

They took a religious census and found only six *un*saved people in the area — and they were regarded as "gospel-hardened." Yet in only two years, the Christian believers of that church led over three hundred people to Christ. Their church attendance jumped to nearly four hundred.

That young pastor knew the secret of winning the *un*converted. He knew that the *un*saved would not usually come to church to get saved.

They had to be reached with the message of Christ — *out where they are.*

He trained some of the church members to witness for Christ. They began knocking on doors, presenting the Gospel to people and leading them to Christ.

They limited themselves to within twenty-five miles of their church. In two years they were operating three big buses and were hauling over two hundred people weekly to their church.

✧ ✧ ✧

IN A LARGER city, a church had won forty people to Christ within one year. They were not satisfied so they conducted a two-week soulwinning training course. The pastor and his congregation set a goal to evangelize "the world of our community."

Within two months that church had gone outside their sanctuary and had won scores of people to Christ. Sixty-seven new families had been brought into their church fellowship.

✧ ✧ ✧

A TRAINING COURSE on soulwinning was conducted in another church in a large metropolitan area.

On Sunday following their training session, the pastor announced that they were dismissing their Sunday evening service. They would go out and witness to the *un*saved. The result was so good that they decided to continue the program for three more nights. The spirit of biblical soulwinning caught fire and a program of house to house evangelism was begun.

The church was stunned by the results achieved. In less than three months, they had won more than two hundred souls to Jesus Christ. The members were not only overwhelmed but their church was overflowing.

✧ ✧ ✧

IN A TOWN of 45,000 people, a church set aside three weeks for an intensive soulwinning campaign in order to evangelize their city.

The first week was given entirely to training the Christians on how to witness of Christ and how to lead a soul to accept Jesus as savior.

The men witnessed, person to person, in jails, rescue missions, flop houses and slum areas. The women visited in the hospitals, women's prisons, shelters, homes for the elderly and other convalescent centers, going from room to room, from bed to bed and from chair to chair.

The main thrust of their efforts was focused on house to house evangelism. Each evening Christians were assigned different streets. They went into the homes to witness and persuaded *un*churched people to accept Christ on the spot.

Within two weeks, three hundred and thirty-three people had embraced Christ as savior and during the next three weeks, that church received over a hundred and fifty new converts into its fellowship.

That pastor said that his people have become so enthusiastic about house to house evangelism that they visit every home in the city every three months.

✧ ✧ ✧

A YOUNG STUDENT on holiday vacation from college attended a church training session on personal soulwinning and enthusiastically embraced the idea. He returned to college and organized a group of ten fellow students into a soulwinning group for the purpose of witnessing to *non*-Christians.

Within one month that group of young students had led more than fifty souls to Christ.

✧ ✧ ✧

THE PASTOR OF another church heard about a program of soulwinning and requested literature in order to train believers in the ministry of witnessing to the *un*converted. They had received only two additions to their church in the past year.

Following their training program, they began to evangelize—outside their church, witnessing of Christ from house to house. Within a year that small church had won to Christ over a hundred lost souls in their community.

✧ ✧ ✧

A CHRISTIAN PROFESSOR who taught at a Bible College recounted a personal experience.

He realized that Christians must get out among *un*saved people in order to effectively witness to them; that the church could not wait for *un*converted people to come to the sanctuary to be saved. So he decided that he would make a definite test of soulwinning *out where the people are*.

He took a group of seven young Christian workers and they went into a certain city. They devoted two hours during three afternoons to house to house visitation and witnessing of Christ.

In three days, they had knocked on the doors of three hundred and ninety-two houses and had been able to talk with a hundred and ninety-eight people. Twenty-four souls had accepted Christ during those three days.

✧ ✧ ✧

FIRST CENTURY CHRISTIANS practiced two kinds of evangelism. In our next chapter, we shall look at them and at Christ's instructions about segregated areas.

Chapter 9

Born In A Blaze

I WAS ONLY TWELVE years old when I was converted. From that day, I wanted to be a soul-winner; I wanted to share with people what Jesus Christ meant to me. I was the seventh son of my parents. My father was the seventh son of his parents. I was raised on a farm where we all worked hard.

Lonnie, one of my older brothers, was converted at an old fashioned Oklahoma brush arbor meeting. There was such a change in him that I became very interested. He took me to a revival meeting in the little town of Mannford. That night I received Jesus Christ as my savior. I started doing whatever I could to witness to *un*converted people in my area.

With a toy press that I received as a Christmas present, I printed Bible verses on scraps of paper—my first tracts, and distributed them among the town's people, a population of not more than three hundred. I never dreamed that within a few years we would be publishing gospel literature in a hundred and thirty-two languages at a rate of more than a ton per working day.

I started preaching at the age of sixteen. Daisy and I were married when we were seventeen and eighteen years old and we became missionaries in India at the ages of twenty and twenty-one. I have preached face to face to millions of people in over eighty nations of the world.

The more I study the Bible and the further I travel in evangelism, the more I am convinced that the greatest ministry possible for a Christian believer is to lead someone to faith in Christ.

In this book, I am sharing *seven reasons why we are soulwinners.*

Two Kinds Of Evangelism

In the book of Acts, First Century believers witnessed of Christ and shared His teachings both *publicly* and from *house to house*. Occasionally, multitudes came together to hear one of them speak or preach, especially if some outstanding healing miracle had occurred.[Ac.3:1-11,5:12-16,8:5-8,9:33-34,14:8-11] But each individual's ministry was in person to person encounters with people.

The book of Acts begins with a reflection on *all that Jesus **began** both to do and teach.*[Ac.1:1] His life was the inspiration and model for First Century

Christians. He had said to those who followed Him, *Whoever believes on me, the works that I do shall he or she do also; and greater works than these shall they do; because I go to my Father.*[Jn.14:12] They believed His words. Their focus was to **continue** doing and teaching what He had **begun** to do and teach. They understood that He was living and ministering *through them*. They were His voice, His feet, His body. He was now *continuing* what He had **begun** but now He was doing it **through them**.

Just before the Lord Jesus ascended back to the Father, He told His followers where to go and what to do: *You shall receive power, after that the Holy Ghost is come upon you: and you shall be witnesses unto me both in Jerusalem, and in all Judea, and in Samaria, and to the uttermost part of the earth.*[Ac.1:8]

A First Century map indicates what this means: *Jerusalem* represents our hometown. *All Judea* suggests our state, province or nation.

No Discrimination

But why did He make special mention of *Samaria* since He had already said *in all Judea* which included *Samaria*. He specified *Samaria* because it was a segregated area. Remember how the woman of Samaria remarked to Jesus, *The Jews have no dealings with the Samaritans.*[Jn.4:9] And the

Jews slandered Jesus saying: *Say we not well that you are a Samaritan, and have a devil?* Jn.8:48

Jesus told His followers to reach *all Judea,* then He specified *and Samaria* — the forgotten, hurting, *un*loved people. Samaria could be Indian or Aboriginal reservations, minority communities, migrant settlements, ghettos, rehabilitation centers, immigrant and refugee communities or any place that is considered inferior or is segregated from the mainstream of society. Obviously God is interested in marginal people as much as He is in any other level of human society. He wants *no one* excluded. Our mission is to reach *every creature.*

After specifying the various sectors of our own region and nation, then He added, *and unto the uttermost part of the earth.* In other words, He was saying, "At home and abroad." Soulwinning is the *worldwide* mission of every believer.

The noted Canadian missionary statesman, Oswald J. Smith said, "*Everyone should either go or send a substitute,*" meaning that we can *all* have a part in communicating the gospel to our world.

The First Century Church practiced *public* evangelism and *personal* evangelism. For more than a half-century, Daisy and I consecrated the very best of our lives and of our energies to follow the example of those Early Church believers.

In public mass evangelism together, we have shared the gospel with millions face to face who have converged on great fields or parks or stadiums where our crusades have been celebrated. But what about the additional millions in the same region who never attended our meetings. We came to realize that mass evangelism could only reach those who came to our crusades. It would never reach those who were not present.

We thought about radio and television evangelism and realized that those media also could only reach the few fortunate enough to have a radio or a television set. They would never communicate the gospel to the millions who were too poor or too primitive to have access to them.

The Way To Reach Everyone

Personal evangelism is the only way to assure that *every creature* is reached by the gospel of Christ. Even those who may not be persuaded to accept Him as their savior can, nevertheless, be given a personal witness of His love.

The Moody Bible Institute has estimated that less than five percent of Christians have led a soul to Christ and that less then ten percent of people in Christian nations attend church.

God never said, "Go, you *unconverted*, to my house and be saved, lest you die." But He did say, *Go you* [believers]...*to every creature.*Mk.16:15

85

Paul the apostle was that kind of a believer. *He reasoned...with the Jews and with the Gentiles...and* **in the marketplace daily** *with those who happened to be there.*[Ac.17:17NKJV]

From The Gallery To The Arena

Personal soulwinning lifts Christian believers out of the gallery of spectators — of **hearers** *of the word,* and places them out in the arena of action as **doers** *of the word.*[Ja.1:22-25]

There is no experience in the church more exhilarating than to look across the aisle at a new believer whom you personally led to Christ. Jesus was allowed to express Himself *through you* in a way that that person responded and received Him as savior. No church can be ineffective when members like that are scattered throughout its congregation.

The First Century Church was born in a blaze of personal soulwinning. A revival of that passion is sweeping the world today as Christians are writing the last chapter of the *Acts of the Believers* before Christ's return.

In the next seven chapters of this book I am sharing *seven reasons why we are soulwinners:*

1. *Because Jesus was.*

2. *Because the harvest is so great.*

3. *Because the laborers are so few.*

4. *Because Jesus said to do it.*

5. *Because of the unfulfilled prophecies concerning Christ's return.*

6. *Because we do not want the blood of non-believers on our hands.*

7. *Because of what we have experienced.*

SOULWINNING

Reason For Soulwinning

I

JESUS
WAS A
SOULWINNER

SINCE CHRIST CAME *to seek and to save that which was lost,*^{Lu.19:10} to be like Christ—a Christian, is to be first and foremost a *Winner of Souls.* After that, one may be a pastor, a musician, a singer, a prophet or prophetess, a teacher, or exercise whatever gift one may have received from God. But it is always a Christian—like Christ *first.* His mission does not change when He comes to live in the believer.

⟫▶

Chapter 10

The Greatest Calling

WE ARE SOULWINNERS, *BECAUSE THAT IS WHAT JESUS WAS.* The Bible says: *This is a faithful saying, and worthy of all acceptation. That Christ Jesus came into the world to save sinners.*[1Ti.1:15] It also says, *The Son of man is come to seek and to save that which was lost.*[Lu.19:10]

Jesus came to save people. That was, and is His mission. First and last, He was a soulwinner—the greatest one the world has ever known!

Christ told the first group of disciples whom He chose: *Follow me, and I will make you fishers of people.*[Mt.4:19] The last group who followed Him to the mount where He ascended back to the Father, heard Him say: *Go make disciples of all nations.*[Mt.29:19] *You shall be my witnesses unto the uttermost part of the earth.*[Ac.1:8]

First and foremost, Jesus was a soulwinner. That is why He came *to save* people. That is why He lived, died, rose again, and sent back the Holy

Spirit to His followers, giving them power to witness for Him with signs and miracles that would confirm that He is alive again.[Ac.1:8]

The word *Christian* means to be *like Christ*. He came to save people, to seek out the lost. To be Christians, we are to be soulwinners like Him.

Christ is born in us and He wills to do the same *in* and *through* us that He did when He ministered on this earth. Yet, there are hundreds of thousands of Christians who have never known the joy of allowing Him to win a soul through them. There are preachers and Bible teachers who have never led a soul to accept Christ. Missionaries have told us that they never won a soul to Christ during their years of ministry abroad.

People Touching People

Jesus took His message to the people. He went wherever they could be encountered — in marketplaces, in streets and roadways, on mountain sides, by seashores, in private homes.

He was criticized by the religious leaders for identifying with the kinds of people who needed His love and compassion. They complained: *This man receives sinners, and eats with them.*[Lu.15:2] He mixed with people, witnessed to them, convinced them and won them. He was not a holier-than-thou type, a religious snob, aloof and sanctimonious.

Jesus lived in rapport with the common people. They were His reason for being in this world. His purpose is our purpose. His mission is our mission. His plan is our plan. He came to save people. We are here in this world for the same purpose.

Jesus said, *For this cause I came into the world, to bear witness of the truth.*[Jn.18:37] That is why we are in our world. Jesus said, *As my Father has sent me, even so send I you.*[Jn.20:21] We are to bear witness of the truth of the gospel, just as He came to *bear witness of the truth.* He said, *I am the way, the truth and the life.*[Jn.14:6]

The Lord Jesus encouraged His followers to *go out into the highways and hedges, and compel them to come in, that my house may be filled.*[Lu.14:23]

He never said, "Go ring a church bell and pray for people to come." He said, "Go out and find hungry and needy people. Win them. Compel them to come to the banquet, that my house may be full."[Lu.14:23] And every follower of His did just that.

After Christ's ascension, His followers continued doing what He had been doing. They stayed busy witnessing in the markets, on the streets, in houses, at public wells, talking, reasoning, witnessing, persuading, preaching, winning souls, compelling people to believe the gospel and to come into the Kingdom of God.

In fact they reminded the public so much of Christ, the man from Nazareth, that critics contemptibly nicknamed them *CHRIST-i-ans.* Those who became His followers imitated His way of life. They taught and lived and acted like Jesus Christ. And they were like Him in winning souls.

That is why we are soulwinners: Because Jesus was. First Century Christians followed their Lord's example. They were busy in their Lord's service *daily* the same as the world's sports arenas, cinemas, casinos, race tracks, bars, amusement parks and discos.

Contemporary Witnessing

Christians today are becoming aware of these principles and are recapturing the zeal and passion of the First Century Church. They are sharing the good news of Jesus Christ with the *un*converted and millions are receiving the gospel.

It has been reported that a certain sect has increased their membership during the last fifty years more than any other religious body. While traditional churches were losing members, this sect was consistently swelling their numbers. What was their secret?

From their inception, they exploited the most strategic method of First Century believers. They encouraged every sect member to be a door to door, person to person witness of their faith.

While traditional Christians occupied their church pews, the members of this active sect used their shoe leather. While fundamental Christians beat a path to their sanctuaries, those sectarian devotees beat a path to the homes of people—visiting them and converting them to their persuasions.

When they gather their new recruits for training, their techniques of witnessing are rehearsed until each new adherent becomes a self-confident and proficient witness.

They make their converts out where the *uncon*-verted people can be found, in private homes, in parks, in offices, in apartment complexes, carrying an audio or video cassette player and armed with attractive literature. They systematically work each section of a town until every family has been contacted. Then they re-begin the same process—and they never quit. They take their message to the people. They never wait for the people to come to their meeting places.

That is exactly what First Century Christians did. They conceived no other way of witnessing for Christ. To them, when they embraced Him as their Lord, their life had one purpose—to share His love and His salvation with others.

The World Waits

The general public is confused about spiritual values. Many people search for direction, but are not sure which church group they can trust. They are streaming to psychologists and psychiatrists, serving as human guinea pigs for every new theory that is conceived by the growing wave of psychotherapists.

Children are confused. Teenagers are adrift. Parents are bickering. Insecurity and dismay ravage the home. Alcoholism, brutality, abuse and perversion are substituted for harmony, love and stability in family life.

Sickness, disease, mental stress, and spiritual emptiness go unattended. Wretched existences are endured behind the doors of many seemingly affluent homes today.

Through those doors is an open world of ministry for Christians. They will discover that the only way we can serve God is by serving people. We reach God when we reach people. We touch God when we touch people. We exalt God when we lift people. We discover God when we discover the infinite value of people.

Mother Teresa of Calcutta, India said, *"Because I cannot see Christ, I cannot express my love to Him in person. But my neighbors I can see, and I can do for them what I would love to do for Jesus if He were visi-*

ble. We are His co-workers — a fruit bearing branch of His vine."

Many people only pray for the *unconverted* to be saved. Jesus said, Go out and bring them in. They will be lost if we only pray for them. Christ wants to speak His love to them *through us*. We are His voice, His expressions, His representatives, His interpreters today.

Tradition has taught us that *evangelists* are the qualified soulwinners; that ordinary believers can only relate to those who are already saved.

A Christian First

A pastor said, "Oh, I'm not a soulwinner. I never could deal with *non*-Christians. My calling is to pastor, to shepherd the flock."

Who is the greatest Shepherd? Jesus! He is also the greatest soulwinner. Every pastor can follow His example.

Another person told me, "Oh, no! I do not invite people to make public decisions for Christ. That is not my calling. My gift is to teach the word of God."

Who is the greatest Teacher? Jesus! He is also the world's greatest soulwinner. Every Christian teacher can follow Christ's example of teaching in a way that convinces people about Him.

My wife, Daisy and I became soulwinners because Jesus was. Paul said, *Christ Jesus came into the world to save sinners.*[1Ti.1:15] He is our example.

A preacher said to me: "Oh, reaching the *un*-converted is not my calling at all. My gift is to teach prophecy." But who is the greatest Prophet? Jesus! And He is a soulwinner.

A minister friend dared to say, "I teach types and shadows from the Old Testament. I'm not a soulwinner. I minister to the Church." But who did that better than Jesus? And He won souls when He taught.

Before anyone could be a pastor, that person had to be a Christian—*like Christ*. First, one is called as a Christian to win souls. Then, one may be called to pastor or to shepherd a flock. Every pastor can be a soulwinner because that is being *like Christ*.

Before anyone could be a Bible teacher, he or she had to be a Christian. After that, one may become gifted as a teacher. But before being gifted to preach or to teach in the church, that person was called as a Christian—to be *like Christ*—like Him in winning souls.

Since Christ, *is come to seek and to save that which was lost,*[Lu.19:10] then to be like Christ—a Christian, is to be first and foremost a *Winner of Souls*. After that, one may be a pastor, a musician, a singer, a prophet or prophetess, a teacher, or exercise whatever gift one may have received from God. But it is always a *Christian — like Christ FIRST*. The mission of Jesus does not change when He comes to live in a believer.

Three Witnesses

This is a principle in the kingdom of God. Here are three witnesses of this fact.[Lu.15:1-19]

— **W**ITNESS ONE: *There is more joy in heaven over one sinner that repents than over ninety-nine persons who need no repentance.*[Lu.15:7]

Heaven rejoices when someone lost has been found. One person who is won to Christ is a greater delight to the Father than ninety-nine saved people. In the Kingdom of God, the priority is on finding and bringing to repentance those who are lost.

— **W**ITNESS TWO: In the kingdom of heaven, the good shepherd is pictured *leaving the ninety-nine* in the fold and going *out into the mountains,* out in the dangerous places, out in the world, to seek and to find the *lost* sheep.[Lu.15:4] The good shepherd does not stay in the fold, caring for the secure flock. He goes out after the one who has been lost. Christ, the good shepherd now does that *through us.*

~WITNESS THREE: A woman has lost a prized coin from her valuable collection. She is not pictured sitting in her comfortable chair, counting and polishing her collection of coins. But rather, she seeks *diligently till she finds* the *lost coin.*Lu.15:8

If that woman's lost coin represents the *un*converted, the scene can be quite different in some places today. Sunday morning, the pastor may polish the *coins* which are safe in the fold—the church members. During the week, they may be polished again. But the *lost coins* are not sought after.

Sunday after Sunday, there may be more polishing of the coins which are already safely guarded. Week after week, more ministry may be directed to the already saved ones.

A teacher may arrive who is gifted to expound the word of God to Christians. Then the polishing may be repeated every night during a series of meetings. Still there may be no ministry to the *non*-Christians—the *un*converted—the *lost* coins.

Then a prophecy teacher may arrive. Still no attention may be given to the *un*converted. Then someone may hold a series of special meetings to teach on spiritual gifts, or on the types and shadows of the Old Testament. Still there may be no outreach to *non*-Christians.

Then singers may come to entertain the Christians, followed by more *polishing*. The *lost coin* may still not be sought. The *lost sheep* may still not be gone after.

Christ cannot reach the *un*converted if Christians do not go after them. The *un*saved world only sees Christ and His love through His followers. He yearns to save the lost, but He can only do it through those in whom He lives.

God never called anyone to any ministry that was not a soulwinning ministry. The very essence of being a Christian is Christ living *in* you — witnessing and ministering *through* you.

✧ ✧ ✧

WHATEVER YOUR TALENT in the church, you are first of all a soulwinner — a *witness*, then you may be a writer, teacher, pastor, prophet, or exercise whatever gift God has blessed you with.

You can be a soulwinner — a real *CHRIST-i-an*, **Because That Is What Jesus Was.**

SOULWINNING

Reason For Soulwinning

II

THE HARVEST
IS SO
GREAT

SINCE CHRIST WAS *moved with compassion* when He saw the multitudes and since we are like Christ, we also are moved with compassion for those who are *un*touched by the gospel. To be *like Christ*, we become involved in God's work, sharing the gospel with our hurting world. ⇒

Chapter II

Out Where The People Are

WE ARE SOULWINNERS, *Because The Harvest Is So Great.* No one can look into the faces of people who are bewildered by superstitions and religions, as we have done, without doing their utmost to witness to those people about the gospel of Jesus Christ.

For over a half century my wife and I have stood on crude platforms out in open parks, fields and other terrains, before multitudes of under-privileged people including lepers, demoniacs, witch doctors, and sufferers of all kinds of diseases. We have ministered the good news of Christ to them when it was all we could do to hold back tears of human emotions.

Worldwide, there are millions who have not yet been touched by the gospel. They constitute the vast, ripened harvest of souls waiting to be reaped for Christ.

This is the second reason why we are soulwinners: **Because the harvest is so great**.

The Bible says: *When Jesus saw the multitudes, he was moved with compassion on them, because they fainted, and were scattered abroad, as sheep having no shepherd.*Mt.9:36

Pondering these needy multitudes, He said, *The harvest truly is plenteous.*Mt.9:37

What did He do about it? He called *twelve* disciples, gave them power to cast out devils and to heal the sick, and sent them out to help reap this harvest. Later, He chose *seventy* more. Then before His ascension, He conferred upon *all believers* the power to witness Ac.1:8 with evidence — *with signs following,*Mk.16:20 in His name.

Jesus did something about this ripened harvest. He did not just sit and ponder and pray about it. He set about choosing laborers and sending them out into the harvest fields.

Prayer—Then Action

Since Christ was *moved with compassion* when He saw the multitudes and since we are like Him, we also are moved with compassion for those who are *un*touched by the gospel. Because we are *like Christ*, we become involved doing something about sharing His love and His message with these millions.

This truth cannot be over emphasized: *We are Christ's body; He can only reach people through us.*

First Century Christians went to those who did not know Christ, *expounding and testifying the kingdom of God, persuading them concerning Jesus...from morning till evening.*^{Ac.28:23} They were busy in the market places, on street corners, at village wells, by the seaside, in the homes of people—wherever *un*converted people could be encountered.

Principle Of Evangelism

People do not go fishing in their bathtubs. To catch fish, they cast their nets out in the streams, lakes, and waterways—*out where the fish are.*

Farmers never harvest their crops inside their dining rooms or banquet halls. To reap the ripened grain, they wield their sickles through the heat of the day, away from the house, out in the broad fields—*out where the grain is ripe and ready to be harvested.*

The best place to win souls is not inside church sanctuaries. To reap the *un*converted, believers experience their greatest success when they take their witness of Christ out beyond their sacred church walls, out into the *un*sacred markets, onto the streets, in jails, hospitals, houses of prostitution, in private homes,—*out where unconverted people live, work and play. This is evangelism.*

Paul asked, *How shall* [the *unconverted*] *believe on Christ of whom they have not heard? and how shall they hear without a preacher* [a witness]?[Ro.10:14]

Reaching People
Where They Are

We have invested over five decades of our lives reaching people *out where they are*. This is why we build our platforms out in parks, on race tracks or stadium grounds, or out on broad public fields.

Hindus or Moslems do not go into church buildings or enter Christian temples. Shintoists and Buddhists do not frequent places of Christian worship. *Un*converted people do not generally attend churches.

But when believers take the gospel out to public places — to seasides, parks, stadiums, race tracks or open fields, the *un*converted come by the tens of thousands — Moslems, Hindus, Buddhists, — *non*-Christians.

After we have won them *out where they are* and after they have been converted, then they are eager to come into places of Christian worship to learn more about Christ and His word.

The Early Church went out where the people were. That was where Peter and John shared their testimony with the crippled man who was healed.[Ac.3:1-11; 4:4]

That was where Peter's mass meetings were held in Jerusalem—out in the streets and busy roadways.[Ac.5:12-16]

That was where Philip preached to all of Samaria—out in the public. That is where he encountered the Ethiopian eunuch and led him to Christ—out on the trader's roadway.[Ac.4:4-8]

That was where Paul convinced the philosophical Greek people about Christ—out in the midst of *Mars hill*.[Ac.17:22]

That was where he ministered Christ's miracle love *[amidst] the barbarous people on the island called Melita,*[Ac.28:1-2] out among those who had never heard the gospel before.

Observe The Farmer

Being raised on a farm, one of thirteen children, I know what a ripened harvest looks like. I know the urgency of a field of grain that is ready to be harvested. When the grain was ripe, we toiled from early until late, to save the precious fruit of our labor before a storm might destroy it. We did that *out in the fields where the grain had grown.*

From early in the morning, the laborers toiled to save the grain. Then they would go to the house where a good meal was served to nourish their weary bodies. After eating, they returned to the fields to continue reaping, day after day, until the farthest corners of each field was harvested.

But this urgency of saving the grain while it is ripe does not usually motivate Christians today. If a program of soulwinning evangelism is scheduled, it often consists of little more than special prayer meetings where members implore the Holy Spirit to draw people into their church sanctuary to be converted. This is not the way a reaper saves a field of grain.

Such an idea is good for the few who may be drawn to the church and converted. But the ripened harvest of our hurting world will never be reached inside sanctuary walls simply because the masses of *un*converted people will never be there.

If we want to reap the harvest of our generation, the secret is in *rediscovering the passion and zeal of the First Century Church*. Those believers went out into cities and villages in constant pursuit of lost souls — at the risk of their lives. This is Christianity in action. This is being *Christlike*.

"Oh God, Save The Grain!"

Let us paint a simple hypothetical picture. As farmers, suppose we had eaten a good meal at noon, then, with our bodies nourished, suppose we had pondered the beauty and the challenge of ripened field of grain. Storm clouds were gathering. The rumble of thunder and the flash of lightening threatened the grain.

Suppose we had knelt for a long afternoon of prayer, asking God to send forth His Holy Spirit to reap the golden harvest and to save the grain? Would He have done it?

Or, suppose we had earnestly prayed: "Oh, Lord, save this grain. Send it to us. Let your Holy Spirit draw it to us so that we can reap it here in the comforts of our beautiful family home." Would He have done it? Would not that prayer sound somewhat absurd?

Most Christians have never gone outside their church sanctuary to reap any of the ripened soul-harvest of their area. Instead, they pray inside their church building: "Oh, God, draw lost souls into our church so that we can teach them the gospel and lead them to Christ." The masses of *un*converted people will not be saved that way.

Getting God's Viewpoint

Preachers and Bible teachers often convince Christians that believers are *holy,* and that *un*converted people are *unholy.* Therefore believers should not jeopardize the sanctity of their spirituality by mixing with "sinners." Rather than to go out among the *un*saved, out in *un*sacred places, it is better to gather in the sanctuary and to pray for God to send lost people to them to be saved.

But the misconception is serious. Human persons are *all* holy — those who are saved and those who are *un*saved. *Everyone* is sacred in God's eyes. Christians do not have a higher value than *non*-Christians. The same price has been paid by Christ for the redemption of *unconverted* people as was paid for *converted* people.

The only difference in believers and *un*believers is that Christians have been made aware of the price that has been paid to ransom them; they have been informed about the love that God has for them. But *unconverted* people do *not* know these facts. Therefore, the mission of believers is to inform the *un*informed of God's love. When they know these facts, they can believe them and be saved.

Mixing With The *Un*converted

But sanctimonious church members seem to imply: "We dare not be seen witnessing to people of questionable reputation. Our rapport in these lower levels of society could bring dishonor to our church and to our Lord's name.

Many traditional Christians seem to be saying: "Here in our sacred sanctuary, the dignity of our church is not compromised. We will pray, and if God sends *unconverted* people _to us_ here in our sacred environment, we can lead them to faith in Him."

But should Christians wait for *un*converted people to come to their church to be saved? Should believers not rather take Christ's message to the unsaved, *out where they live and work and play?* Our Lord came to our world where we are, dirty and unclean as we had made it. He did not sink to our level, but He lifted us to His. That is what He wills to do through us for others.

Each–Reach–Teach

In the First Century Church, the followers of Christ were His witnesses. They were soulwinners. They went out in the highways and hedges and compelled people to come in, *so that His house might be filled.*

Believers are to win people *out where they are.* Then they will come into a worship center, under the leadership of a pastor where Bible teachers can help them to *grow in grace, and in the knowledge of our Lord and Savior Jesus Christ.*[2Pe.3:18] There they will *increase and abound in love one toward another, and toward all people.*[1Th.3:12] As a result, they also will soon join the reapers in saving those who are lost.

Ideas For Soulwinners

There are many ways to reach people and to share Christ. You might consider buying or renting a small tent, a hall, a shop or a room; then invite a few Christians to share with you. Equip them with literature and other tools—videos, films, tapes or cassettes.

Invest in portable audio or video cassette players. Invite fellow-believers to take one, equipped with recorded sermons, music, and gospel literature, and witness out in the streets, in homes or play areas, in bars, at beaches or in businesses.

If you are fortunate enough to be part of a soulwinning church, present these ideas to your pastor. Share this vision so that Christlike leaders can be involved and prepared to nourish new believers in the faith of Christ.

As soon as Jesus had cast the demons out of the naked demoniac, and as soon as that man had the chance to hear Christ's words and to believe on Him, Jesus arranged for some garments to be acquired to clothe him properly.

The villagers were astonished as *they came to Jesus and saw him that was possessed with the devil, and had the legion, sitting, and clothed, and in his right mind.*Mk.5:15

Ten Harvest Fields For You

Jesus sent the man, as His witness, to the ten towns called the Decapolis.[Mk.5:19-20 LB] He was told to *go home to your friends, and tell them how great things the Lord has done for you and has had compassion on you.*[Mk.5:19LB] *And he departed, and began to publish in Decapolis how great things Jesus had done for him: and all people did marvel.*[Mk.5:20LB] He was just a new convert, but he became a powerful witness for Christ.

The Lord may have ten supermarkets for you to reach, or ten convalescent homes, ten streets, ten counties or provinces, ten villages, ten communities or ten households or families. For me, it has already been over eighty different nations.

Soulwinning Strategies

Imprint your church name on each tract or book that you distribute. Encourage each worker to go out where the people are to witness and to win them to Christ. Encourage them to pray for the sick, and to expect the Lord to confirm their witness *with signs following.*[Mk.16:20]

During the day, believers can canvass each area, leading souls to Christ in their own homes.

At night, they can preach or teach or use their audio or video cassettes or films and win souls in whatever kind of public meetings they have been able to arrange.

On Sundays, these Christian workers can bring their newly won converts and families to church where the pastor can nourish them in God's word. They can become effective soulwinners in their areas like the man of Gadera did after his encounter with Jesus.

Some Christians will go into jails and prisons, others into hospitals (with headsets for their cassette players so they will not disturb other patients). Others will go into convalescent homes and to other special areas of need.

Youth groups, supplied with cassettes, books, tracts, and musical instruments, can witness on street corners, in residential areas, in shopping centers, in market places—wherever there are people, *out where they live and work and play.*

Our Motto—Our Mission

Christ can only show His love to people through Christians who believe in His love enough to tell about it. Remember that each believer is Christ's body in action today and that He can only reach the lost through those who will allow Him to speak and touch and see and hear and embrace through them.

Paint a large banner and hang it inside your church or classroom where everyone can see it:

> *Our Motto*: **Every Christian, A Witness!**
> *Our Mission*: **Out Where the People Are!**

Banners are effective. When we attended Dr. Oswald J. Smith's evangelism convention in Toronto, Canada many years ago, the atmosphere was alive with banners that filled the spaces on each wall. Sitting there and reading those challenging lines stirred our spirits and greatly inspired us. It is an old technique, but it always works. Did you ever notice how demonstrators brandish banners in their parades?

Throughout the week, engage in a busy program of soulwinning. On Sundays and some midweek evenings, let the witnesses gather at the worship center to be nourished and inspired by God's word. But then let them return in their new strength to witness of Christ among the *un*saved.

Enthusiasm For Action

This is the lifestyle of the happy believer. It gives excitement and purpose to Christian living. It eliminates depression and loneliness. It adds enthusiasm and inspiration to your church. This is evangelism as it was practiced by the First Century Church.

Mushrooming in every city and country, is a generation *un*reached by the gospel. There are many forms of religion, but most of society is *unaware of the reality of Jesus Christ.* Our contemporary world is a ripened harvest. Christ can only reach them through us. We are His body today.

✧ ✧ ✧

DAISY AND I invested over a half century of our lives ministering as a team, reaping this worldwide soul harvest. In every nation, *the Lord has worked with us, confirming the word with signs following.*Mk.16:20 Literally millions have believed on Christ in our crusades. Now I am privileged to continue the vast outreaches of this international evangelism ministry. This is the heartbeat of biblical Christianity.

The second reason we are soulwinners: ***Because The Harvest Is So Great.***

Reason For Soulwinning

III

THE
LABORERS
ARE
SO FEW

WHILE NINE TENTHS of the world's gospel ministers are preaching in relative comfort to Christians of industrialized nations, the other ten percent of preachers are trying to meet the spiritual needs of ninety-one percent of our planet's population living in emerging nations. This is not fair.

Chapter 12

Here Am I! Send Me!

WE ARE SOULWINNERS, *Because The Laborers Are So Few.*

*Also I heard the voice of the Lord, saying, Whom shall I send, and who will go for us? Then said I, **Here am I; send me**.*[Is.6:8]

World population is increasing by tens of millions of people each year. The gospel barely touches ten percent of that annual population increase.

A big percent of the world's present population—billions of souls alive today, including tribes who speak over a thousand languages, have *never* heard the gospel.

In Japan, after over four hundred years of traditionally tenuous and ineffectual church ministry, the overwhelming majority of their teeming millions of people are still *non*-Christian, *un*touched by the message of Christ.

Most of Japan's ninety-five thousand rural communities still have no Christian witness. Yet, there is a tremendous response to the gospel in Japan wherever people are given the opportunity to hear it, especially among the youth. Those engaged in literature, radio and television evangelism receive over half of their responses from the fifteen to twenty-five-year age group. *Young Japan is ripe for harvesting.*

About one out of three people today live in China where gospel ministry has been severely restricted for decades. The spiritual hunger of the people is evidenced by the fact that almost two million Chinese men or women commit suicide annually.

Moslems send thousands of Islamic teachers to nations south of the African Sahara each year. They were converting the people to Islam faster than Christians were winning them to Christ. But in recent decades, the gospel has been promulgated with such rapidity in certain nations of Africa that the tide has now changed in favor of Christianity .

This should motivate gospel believers more and more to take advantage of this epochal opportunity to reap this vast human harvest with renewed enthusiasm and dedication.

The World Harvest

Jesus said, *Lift up your eyes, and look on the fields; for they are white already to harvest.*Jn.4:35

He said, *The harvest truly is plenteous, but the laborers are few; pray ye therefore the Lord of the harvest, that he will send forth laborers into his harvest.*Mt.9:37-38

We have looked upon these vast harvest fields. We have prayed for more laborers. But we have done more than that. We have committed the best of our lives to help reap this rich human harvest for the Kingdom of God.

That is one of the principal reasons that we are soulwinners: ***The laborers are so few.***

In India a recent census indicated that not one Christian is living in a district of seventy-seven villages. No national pastor, missionary or evangelist has yet carried a gospel witness of Christ to the people of that area. They live and die without knowledge of God's salvation—not because they have rejected Him, but because during the last two thousand years, not one Christian has shared with them the gospel of God's love.

Imbalance In God's Work

Jesus stressed, *The harvest is ripe, but the laborers are few.* While over nine-tenths of the world's gospel ministers are preaching in relative comfort to Christians of industrialized nations, the other ten percent of preachers are trying to meet the spiritual needs of ninety-one percent of our planet's population living in emerging nations. This is not fair.

Following Paul's example, we have chosen to give the best of our lives to sharing Christ where the need is greatest and where the laborers are fewest. The apostle said: *I have strived to preach the gospel, not where Christ was named, lest I should build upon another man's foundation.*[Ro.15:20]

That is why we have tried to multiply our lives by producing and providing *Tools For Evangelism* for the Church of this century, in nations abroad.

The Voice That Duplicates

By recording our proven gospel messages on magnetic tape, on video cassettes and on film, then by having them interpreted into national languages and dialects, we are reaching thousands of *un*evangelized villages, tribes and areas simultaneously.

When a national Christian, who has not yet developed his or her own preaching skills, switches on a audio-cassette unit, *a new soulwinner is in the making*. After that worker has broadcasted our messages to others for a few weeks, listening each time and being exposed to our presentation of the gospel, he or she can usually proclaim those truths effectively by themselves. Then their cassette player can be passed on to another inexperienced worker and the process of evangelism and of duplicating another worker is repeated. This procedure has proven effective in nations around the world.

Docu-Miracle Films And Videos

Each time one of our docu-miracle crusade films is shown to a crowd of people in a *non*-Christian nation, *it is another powerful soulwinning tool in action.* Another crowd of people receives the gospel. They see demonstrated how God's word builds faith. They see how a Christian prays to God and how He answers prayer and confirms His gospel with signs, miracles and wonders. As a result, they become followers of Christ. They see the proof that He is a miracle-working Savior and they receive Him. They see clearly that Jesus Christ is more than another foreign religion.

These historic docu-miracle films are produced and provided *in all video formats.*

There are few villages in the free world where one of these miracle-crusade films has not been projected. Most showings result in a new national church being opened in the community.

For over forty years, these dynamic crusade films (now in video formats) have been illustrating in thousands of villages how *non*-Christian areas can be successfully evangelized. They have demonstrated to tens of thousands of national preachers how to effectively present the gospel, how to lead *un*converted people to faith in Christ, and how to minister healing to a crowd of people where hundreds may be sick, diseased or physically impaired. They have literally inspired a worldwide return to apostolic, miracle evangelism in our century.

First Century Faith In Action

These crusade documentaries have proven to be as effective on the home front as they are overseas. Each one demonstrates First Century apostolic ministry being continued in our generation. Healing miracles captured in action are as relevant today as those recorded in the Bible.

These docu-miracles communicate God's word in a way that the full impact of biblical gospel faith in action is perceived.

These crusade films constitute a bridge between the world of biblical antiquity and our world today. They transmit the gospel with the same impact that it had 2,000 years ago, presenting Bible truths with the same authenticity in today's context that it had in its original context.

Probably no soulwinning tool has ever influenced so many millions of people in so many *non-*

Christian nations to embrace faith in the Bible and to receive Jesus Christ as their Lord.

The Powerful Printed Page

Early in our ministry, we realized that the power of the printed page would be almost unequaled by any other evangelism tool

In 1959, I had a compelling experience. I seemed to be looking down from a big airplane upon vast jungles, pondering the *un*reached millions in those areas. Then the Lord impressed me with this question:

"Suppose you were dropped into that vast region knowing that only a few days of time remained and that you were the only messenger of Christ that those people would ever have an opportunity to hear. What would you do? What would you say?"

I responded, *"Lord, every day I would tell them about Jesus—what He came for—how He saved and healed people—how He died and rose again, and why—and how He is now alive and wants to do the same things for them that He did for people in Bible days."*

It was as though I heard the words: "Go, write the things you would tell them. Keep it simple. Publish it on paper and record it on tape. Then spread those simple messages to every village possible. And *hurry!* Because you will be an old man, or I will return before you finish the task."

That experience focused my mission in life.

I knew I could never visit every village in person, but I could multiply the dissemination of the gospel incalculably by recording messages on tapes and by publishing them on paper. Then I could reproduce them by the tons, by the millions. I could develop a vast arsenal of *translingual Tools for Evangelism*. I could fill the hands of tens of thousands of national preachers and gospel workers worldwide with gospel tools in their own languages. We could literally **reach the unreached**. Our life's purpose was clear.

God inspired me to write eighteen brief gospel tracts, and to make each one utterly simple, yet with enough dynamic Bible truth for the recipient to be saved even if it was the only message about Christ that he or she might ever receive.

For years those tracts have been published at the rate of *a ton per working day, in 132 languages*. They are not written for Christians but for the millions of *un*churched people who are waiting in spiritual darkness.

National pastors and leaders around the globe have acclaimed that series of salvation and healing tracts as the best ever provided for their fields. Although written for the *un*reached in villages abroad, they have become favorites across the homefront too because of their direct, simple, gospel message.

Any Christian leader or gospel worker can request that series of tracts, in any language that we possess, and they will be provided for the limited cost of duplicating the eighteen negative sheets (plus handling and postage). Those anointed tracts have seeded the world with the simplicity of the gospel message and they are as effective today as ever.

✧ ✧ ✧

YOU CAN INCREASE your gospel witness by utilizing these *Soulwinning Tools.* You can provide them for national leaders or pastors and gospel workers in nations abroad. And you can put them to work on the homefront, reaching the *un*churched. They afford unmatched opportunities for missionary ministry at home among people of language-groups other than your own. Think about it.

Why are we soulwinners? *Because The Laborers Are So Few.*

SOULWINNING

Reason For Soulwinning

IV

CHRIST'S
GREAT
COMMISSION

JESUS SAID, *Preach to every creature.* If one nation is ninety-five percent Christian while another is ninety-five percent non-Christian, and we want to carry out Christ's plan, the gospel with the non-Christian nation.

If we see ten people lifting a log, nine on the small end and one on the large end—and we want to help, it does not require a special revelation to know where to help lift.

Chapter 13

The Choice To Win

WE ARE SOULWINNERS, *Because Of The Great Commission Of Jesus Christ.*

The last thing Jesus authorized His followers to do before He returned to the Father was: *Go into all the world, and preach the gospel to every creature.*Mk.16:15

This is Christ's authority for each of His followers. This is the great opportunity that He offers believers. This is every Christian's privilege, calling, purpose, and ministry.

When God's love overflowed to the point that He gave His only begotten Son for our redemption, it was for *the whole world,* so that **whoever** *believes in him will not perish, but* will *have everlasting life.*Jn.3:16

The Lord Jesus left us no privilege greater than to announce the gospel to every creature. This is the believer's guarantee of happiness.

This is the mission to which First Century Christians devoted themselves. They understood their calling. They *continued* the same ministry that Christ *began*. They knew He was living in them, doing through them the same things that He did before He was crucified. That is why they were called *CHRIST-i-ans*.

Christ Is *Un*changed Today

Perhaps no couple in this generation has committed themselves so completely to the ministry of world evangelism, for so many decades, as Daisy and I have. It is possible that we have announced the gospel of Christ to more *un*converted people, in *non*-Christian nations, than any couple in human history. BRAGADOCIOUS!

If you had walked on to the grounds of one of our mass crusades back in the late forties or fifties, then if you could attend one of our crusades today, you would hear the same gospel presented with the same simplicity. You would observe the same strategy, hear the same prayers, and you would witness the same spiritual and physical miracles that always confirm the proclamation of the gospel.

Witnessing To Millions
Face To Face

We live and breathe for one purpose: To share the gospel with the greatest possible number of people, by every means at our disposal. We not only use our voices as Christ speaks through us, but we also use the channels of mass media, of reproduction, of duplication, and every form of gospel dissemination that we can employ.

We have conducted almost a steady stream of public gospel crusades throughout the past fifty-five years, preaching face to face to literally millions of *un*converted people in *non*-Christian nations.

But this has not been enough. These mass public meetings only last for two or three hours each day. Long ago, we realized that there are other hours of the day to be utilized?

Reaching Extra Millions

It dawned on us that we could *write* the same messages that we *preach*. Giant presses could reproduce them by the millions—by the tons—in other languages of our world. Doing this, we could reach hundreds of millions of souls who would never hear the sound of our voices.

For years, we averaged publishing over a ton of gospel *tracts* every working day—not counting the additional tons of our *books* and other publications that we have poured out to the nations of the world. This literature has been rolling off the world's presses in *a hundred and thirty-two different languages.*

With millions of people becoming literate every week and with their eager quest for reading materials, the printing of gospel literature opens doors for the Christian Church to reach every *literate* person with the gospel.

In addition to our crusades and literature ministries, we realized that we could still do more. What about the *illiterate* people of our world?

Gospel Duplication

To reach the millions who can neither read nor write, we took advantage of audio and video cassette technology and of cinematography. What fantastic possibilities these technologies presented for personal evangelism and for television and radio outreaches.

So we began to preach the same good news, on film and on tape that we had proclaimed to millions in our crusade audiences. Then we began to create *Tools for Evangelism* to equip national preachers and gospel workers all over the world for reaching the *un*converted masses.

It was not long before the wheels of two additional outreaches were rolling. Our sound production team began duplicating our crusade messages in sight and sound, in scores of languages, with more dialects being added at every possible opportunity.

Today, tens of thousands of audio and video cassettes as well as docu-miracle crusade films, in around seventy major languages, are facilitating national church leaders, evangelists, pastors, and gospel ministers worldwide, for sharing the gospel.

One pastor alone showed one of our docu-miracle films twenty times in one province. He reached over fifty thousand souls and witnessed more than eight thousand new decisions for Christ.

Another minister reported two thousand new decisions for Christ in only eight days of docu-miracle film ministry. These figures are duplicated in nations around the world.

National Missionary Vision

Jesus said, *Preach the gospel to every creature.* We pondered the millions of tribal people living beyond the fringes of civilization, out of the range of missionaries or national church leaders, without television or radio. *These also must hear the gospel.* Over two thousand tribes do not comprehend the languages used by mass media and do not have, or perhaps have never heard of an electronic apparatus for receiving those signals. We were convinced that we must find ways to help reach them too.

In this soul quest, our *National Missionary Evangelism* program was born. The idea occurred to us that we could inspire Christians in prosperous nations to share a monetary gift each month to personally sponsor a national preacher *as a bonafide missionary* to *un*reached tribes in *un*evangelized areas.

Competent Nationals
Christian Sponsors

We communicated our vision to missionary organizations, offering to sponsor trained, qualified national preachers who would go into *un*evangelized areas to teach the gospel and to raise up new churches. As they recruited competent nationals, we recruited Christian sponsors. The balance between the demand and the supply has been a constant miracle since this dynamic program was inaugurated.

We have sponsored more than **thirty-thousand national preachers as full time missionaries** in thousands of *un*reached towns and villages of over a hundred nations. This program has made it possible for these neglected tribes and peoples to hear the gospel of Christ.

Years ago, Daisy and I heard the remarkable missionary statesman, Dr. Oswald J. Smith of Canada. He asked the question: *"Why should anyone hear the gospel twice before everyone has heard it once?"* The answer to that question is, to this day, a pivotal issue in our world ministry.

As a result of our sponsoring those thousands of national preachers as missionaries in *un*reached areas, for many years an average of **over one new church** *per day* **has been established and has become self-supporting**— *almost four hundred new churches per year in previously* **unreached** *areas.* Never in Church history has such a far-reaching evangelism program been undertaken that prioritizes *reaching the UNreached* with the gospel.

Targeting the *UN*reached

Every outreach and program of our world ministry has targeted *non*-Christians — the *un*churched, the *un*evangelized. Jesus said, *My purpose is to invite sinners to turn from their sins, not to spend my time with those who think themselves already good enough.*Lu.5:32 LB

Jesus said, *Preach the gospel to every creature.* To reach them, we must go to them — wherever they are. If one nation is ninety-five percent Christian and another is ninety-five percent *non*-Christian, and we want to carry out Christ's plan, our choice is clear: We minister in the *non*-Christian nation.

If ten people are lifting a log, nine on the small end and one on the large end—and we want to help, we lift on the large end.

If two fields of grain are ripe for harvest, and storms threaten them both, if a hundred reapers are toiling in the small field and only one is reaping in the large field, and if we want to help save the grain, we labor in the field where the need is greatest and the workers are fewest.

Where A Believer's Witness Counts Most

This is why many Christian professionals today are relocating in gospel neglected nations in order to operate their business or profession where it can facilitate them in sharing Christ with people who have not heard the gospel. That way, they can be part of world missions as much as if they were appointed by a missions board.

One of our granddaughters, with her husband and three sons, relocated to Russia because they felt that the people there have a greater need for their gospel than do people in the United States.

One of our grandsons and his Hollander wife are missionary-evangelists. They have conducted large gospel crusades in over fifty nations.

Recently he returned from the interior of Borneo where he witnessed tremendous meetings among tribes who had never before received the message of Jesus Christ.

Another one of our grandsons, with his Argentinean wife, devoted nearly three years of ministry to the nation of Romania, and established three new churches. Then they relocated to Ecuador, South America where their ministry is producing new churches in areas that need the gospel.

Opportunities Worldwide

Christian mechanics, pharmacists, artists, masons, dentists, photographers, plumbers, carpenters, engineers or those with any other profession or skill can relocate to some *un*evangelized nation of their choice. Their profession will be desperately needed and welcomed. While practicing their trade or profession or skill, they can witness to *non-*Christians. They do not have to be ordained ministers to share the gospel. This is the privilege of every believer.

The people in these nations abroad can only experience Christ's love as Christians live and witness among them. Jesus can never reach them without a believer to express Himself through. He is interpreted or represented *in* and *through* those who have received Him. His good news is communicated through believers. He expresses His love through their lips. He touches through their hands and embraces with their arms.

Government And Business Posts

Business opportunities in emerging nations are often grasped by *un*converted people, or by those who have no interest in sharing Christ. With a zest for adventure, they rush through these open doors, establish businesses or agencies abroad, then often practice non-Christian life styles that hinder the progress of the gospel.

Meanwhile, committed Christians of integrity and of high moral standards remain at home, assuming that they need a missionary call before they can go abroad and witness for Christ. They forget that our Lord can only reach people in these emerging nations through human beings in whom He lives.

Dedicated believers are the ones who should take advantage of these opportunities abroad. Their lifestyle in the community where they relocate can contribute to the betterment of the area through the ennobling influence of the Jesus-life. *Righteousness exalteth a nation.*[Pr.14:34]

The *"Call"* To Believers

Christians do not need a special call to do what Christ has authorized them to do. They only need to see the world as God sees it and to accept the fact that they are His chosen ambassadors or representatives in any nation or community where they may choose to establish themselves.

The Lord asks, *Whom shall I send, and who will go for us?* Is.6:8 Any Bible believer concerned about this question can answer with Isaiah: *Here am I, Lord. Send me.*Is.6:8

Every follower of Christ has His authority to go and share the gospel with as many people as he or she can reach. *The call has already been given.* The opportunities are plentiful. The need is urgent. Success is assured. As Christ's ambassador, the Christian believer is authorized to take action as His representative, and needs no further calling.

God's Unfailing Guidance

As you begin to think about your world and as you inform yourself about conditions in various nations, you will be guided by God's Spirit to an area where the opportunity is greatest and the need for Christian messengers is the most urgent.

Paul was enroute to Asia on a certain occasion, when he was suddenly *forbidden of the Holy Spirit.*

Then he tried going into Bithynia: but the Spirit suffered them not...then a vision appeared to Paul in the night. In this vision, *a man of Macedonia prayed him, saying, Come over into Macedonia, and help us.*Ac.16:6-9

When that happened, Paul and his group accepted it as God's guidance for them. *After he had seen the vision, immediately they endeavored to go into Macedonia, assuredly gathering that the Lord had called them to preach the gospel unto them.*Ac.16:10

That is the kind of guidance you can expect to receive, if you keep yourself sensitive to the needs of our world and to the commission of Christ. Paul was already committed to going throughout his world, preaching the gospel. While he was enroute to other *regions beyond,* he received guidance into the *un*reached territory of Macedonia.

Sensitive To *His* Direction

This has happened to us numerous times. Once we were going to India. But enroute, we were impressed of the Lord to change our course and to go into the southern tip of the Philippines. Our obedience resulted in a glorious mass crusade among those needy people. Hundreds of churches are flourishing today that were seeded through that significant evangelism event.

Often we have been guided this way. Usually it happens when we are *in action*. Our constant understanding with our Father is this: *"Lord, if there is any certain field or area or nation where You want to guide us, show us and we will go. But if You do not, we will choose the best opportunity to reap the greatest harvest, where there are the fewest laborers, and we will be there reaping until You guide us elsewhere."*

Jesus said, *Lo, I am with you **alway**.*[Mt.28:20] He is *in* us. We are His body.[1Co.6:19] We go so that He can go. He reaches the people through us. We speak and witness and minister in His name, as His representatives. Our orders are given: *Go into all the world. Preach the gospel to every creature.*[Mk.16:15]

Open Doors

The *un*converted world is hurting. They have problems without answers, diseases without remedies, fears without faith, guilt without pardon, confusion without peace. They constitute our golden opportunity for fulfillment in life, and they guarantee us success, self-esteem and total happiness in life.

As we lift needy people, *we are lifted.* Healing them, *we are healed.* Loving them, *we are loved.* In serving them, *we truly serve our Lord.*

When we stand before Him, He will commend us: *I was hungry and you gave me meat. I was thirsty and you gave me to drink. I was a stranger and you took me in; Naked and you clothed me. I was sick and you visited me. I was in prison and you came to me... Inasmuch as you did it unto one of the least of these... you did it unto me.*Mt.25:35-40

Jesus Christ died for the whole world. His blood was shed for the redemption of every human person.Mt.26:28

But, *how can they call on him if they have not believed? And how can they believe on him if they have not heard?...So then faith* [to be saved or healed or blessed] *comes by hearing...the word of God.*Ro.10:14,17

✧ ✧ ✧

YOU AND I are the witnesses, the confessors, the testifiers, the voices, the preachers, the instruments through which this world *hears* the gospel and discovers Christ. He lives and ministers *through us.*

Our choice has been to share Christ with our hurting world. We are soulwinners, *Because Of The Great Commission Of Jesus Christ.*

Reason For Soulwinning

V

UNFULFILLED PROPHECIES CONCERNING CHRIST'S RETURN

*A*FTER THIS I beheld, and, lo, a great multitude, which no man could number, of all nations, and kindreds, and people, and tongues, stood before the throne, and before the Lamb, clothed with white robes, and palms in their hand; And cried with a loud voice, saying, Salvation to our God which sits upon the throne, and to the Lamb.*Re.7:9-10*

Over a third of the *tongues* of our world have not yet had the gospel published for them. If Christ came today, those hundreds of *kindreds* and *tongues* and *peoples* would not be there crying, *Salvation to our God, and unto the Lamb.* ▬▶

Chapter 14

The Forgotten Ones

WE ARE SOULWINNERS, *Because Of The Unfulfilled Prophecies Concerning Christ's Return.*

For centuries, it has been traditional for Christians to live in anticipation of the Lord's imminent return. Many Bible teachers emphasize that the prophecies concerning Christ's second coming have all been fulfilled .

But is this true? Perhaps the most significant prophecy concerning this event has not yet been fulfilled. It is *THE sign that concerns you and me.* It involves *us* as Christians and *our ministries as His witnesses.*

Jesus specified several *signs of His coming* such as false Christ's, wars, nations in conflict, famines, pestilences, earthquakes, persecutions, deceit, and lack of devotion.^{Mt.24:4-12}

Then He added, *And this gospel of the kingdom shall be preached in all the world for a witness unto all nations; and THEN shall the end come.*Mt.24:14

Christ's last words, before He returned to the Father, were—in essence: *Go now to all nations and proclaim the good news to every creature. As soon as you do this, I shall return.* This significant task has not yet been accomplished. This is the *sign* that concerns *you and me.*

"Come On, Let's Hurry!"

Following Christ's ascension back to the Father, His followers set out to continue what He had begun. I can imagine impetuous Peter nudging John and saying, "Come on, John. Let's hurry. This won't take long. Then our Lord will come back."

The First Century Church understood that not only the apostles, but *each believer was a witness of the resurrection of Jesus Christ.* Day by day—in houses, on streets, at village wells and markets, on roadways—they spread Christ's message and convinced people to believe on Him. Their objective was to reach *every creature* and *all nations* as rapidly as possible—in spite of deadly opposition—because as soon as they finished, Jesus Christ would return.

They knew that Christ had risen from the dead and had returned *to live in them, continuing the*

same works which He did before He was crucified.
They understood that the resurrected Christ
could only speak and witness *through them.* They
remembered His promise to return as soon as the
gospel was *preached in all the world for a witness*
*[with evidence] to all nations.*Mt.24:14

What might have happened if this original zeal
and passion for souls had continued to burn in
the hearts of Christians? But it did not.

It was hundreds of years later before the
Reformation took place and the Church began her
rediscovery of the truths which had been so
cardinal in First Century Christians.

Finally, in the mid-seventeen hundreds, John
Wesley proclaimed the message of spiritual
sanctification. Then followed the Twentieth
Century rediscovery of the baptism of the Holy
Spirit. These were significant steps in *the*
reemergence of effective Christianity.

These vital truths were being unveiled afresh so
that Christians might be empowered to proclaim
the gospel *with signs following* Mk.16:20 in *all the*
world, among *all nations,*Mk.13:10; Lu.24:47 to *every*
*creature.*Mk.16:15 According to what Jesus said, this
must take place before He can come back.Mt.24:14

The Purpose Of Pentecost

But tradition concerning Christ's return blinded the Church to the *Purpose of Pentecost*. (Request information about my book by that title.)

Rather than witnessing with power to the unsaved in houses, on streets, in markets—out where the people are, those early Christians eventually began to wrangle and to split hairs over doctrinal points which caused divisions among them and diverted them from their Lord's commission to keep reaching out to *all nations*.

They left the forgotten ones to their own fate while Christians formed themselves into religious councils to defend their doctrines, proselytizing members and placating themselves with their own religious ceremonies.

Christ's followers had been urged to *Go out quickly into the streets and lanes of the city.*Lu.14:41 *Go out into the highways and hedges.*Lu.14:23 *Go into all the world. Go to every creature.*Mk.16:15 But His words were forgotten, and today, this gospel has not **yet** been preached *as a witness unto all nations* Mt.24:14 as Christ said should be done prior to His return?

It is estimated that over half of our generation has not yet had the opportunity to know about Jesus Christ. They are the forgotten ones of our generation. Dr. Oswald J. Smith's question is more *à-propos* than ever: *"Why should anyone hear the gospel twice before everyone has heard it once?"*

Over a thousand tribes have not yet had a chance to know about Christ's death, burial and resurrection or to know what these events mean to human persons today. Giving the gospel to these people is, therefore, *the* sign which Christ foretold that would indicate His imminent return. But that has not yet been fulfilled.

This prophetic sign *concerns you and me*. We are entrusted with the mission of reaching the *un*reached with the gospel. This is why we are doing everything within our means to win souls and to encourage other Christians worldwide to witness of Christ to the *un*converted.

This is why we have developed an arsenal of *Soulwinning Tools For Evangelism*. This is why we have equipped soulwinners around the world with the *tools* to increase their soul harvest as they share Christ's message with the forgotten ones.

Christ's last commission to us was to accomplish this task. It was the only thing He left us to do.

Revolutionary Strategy

Christians might do well to borrow a page from the political revolutionaries. Have you ever observed how they infiltrate emerging nations?

Their leaders fortify themselves in the mountains or jungles and, from there, impose their domination on local tribes people.

Once entrenched among these forgotten people where disease and poverty are rampant, they organize guerrilla bands and begin their harassment. First, villages; then towns and cities, their target always being destabilization of government.

These insurrectionists go to the very people that the Church has neglected. They pay any price and make any sacrifice to exist in the most difficult areas.

Modern gospel messengers have not been equipped or encouraged to reach these people. In general, they would scarcely survive in such areas, so these tribes have been left without Christ. Whereas, the insurgents send in their teachers to live completely indigenous among them, making the utmost sacrifice — even of life itself, to organize these tribes into forces for their purpose.

Tribes and peoples who have *not* been reached with the gospel *have* been penetrated, influenced and mobilized by despotic propagandists for political purposes.

But Church leaders often convince Christians that all of the prophecies concerning Christ's return are now fulfilled, that believers only need to be faithful in worship and to anticipate His imminent return.

A large church in my home city promoted a TV advertisement, inviting people to come to their church. The advert says, "Christ promises to return for His Church. *Come and wait with us for Him,*" as though all that Christians need to do is to *wait* for Christ to return.

But the fact is that the Church's mission has *not* yet been accomplished. The Bible says *the ever-lasting gospel [will be] preached unto them that dwell on the **earth**, and to every **nation**, and **kindred**, and **tongue**, and **people**.*Re.14:6; 5:9; 7:9 and **THEN** shall the end come.Mt.24:14

The Sign That Concerns You And Me

This is why we are soulwinners, **because this prophecy is still unfulfilled.**

It is the prophecy that concerns *you and me*. Christ died for *every creature.* But He can only reach them through *us.* We are His instrumentality today. He ministers through *us.*

This is why most of our public ministry has been among the *un*churched masses of *non*-Christian nations abroad. There is where the *un*reached of our world can be found. We go to them — out where they are — so that Christ can speak to them *through us.*

155

It would be more convenient to live our lives with the comforts of home. But our opportunity as Christians is to witness to as many souls as we can find ways to encounter.

Our Unfinished Task

Jesus said, *The gospel must first be published among all nations.*Mk.13:10

Sometimes it is argued that: "Every *nation* has already received the gospel at one time or another."

Evidently our Lord knew such voices would be raised so He specified to the Apostle John who would be saved. He said, *I beheld a great multitude, which no person could number, of all nations, and kindreds, and people, and tongues...And they cried with a loud voice, saying, Salvation to our God which sits upon the throne...*Re.7:9-10

This is the multitude of the redeemed, gathered to worship before God's throne. Among this multitude were those from *all nations. Nations* is mentioned first.

Some say, "I'm sure that all *nations* have heard the gospel."

Perhaps, but what John saw was more specific than that. The Holy Spirit specified all *kindreds, and people and tongues.*

If Christ returned today, this scene could not be as John saw it. To be included in that multitude, the people must hear the gospel, believe it, and be redeemed through the blood of the Lamb.

John said, *I saw another angel...having the everlasting gospel to preach unto them that dwell on the earth, and to every nation, and kindred, and tongue, and people.*Re.14:6

But, Paul asks, *how shall they believe in him of whom they have not heard?* Ro.10:14

And how can they hear Christ's gospel if He cannot speak through us?

We are His body today — His lips, His voice. We are to go so that Christ can speak to the people through us. This is how they will hear the *everlasting gospel* and believe it.

Over a thousand *peoples* have not yet heard the gospel, not even once. Christ has not been able to reach them because Christians have not gone to them. We must understand that **He will not send angels to do what He has sent us to do**. Paul said, *The glorious gospel...was* **committed to our trust**.1Ti.1:11 *We are allowed of God to be* **put in trust** *with the gospel.*1Th.2:4 *The gospel...was* **committed unto us**.Ga.2:7

Over a third of the *tongues* (languages) of our world have not yet had the gospel published in them. If Christ returned today, those hundreds of *kindreds* and *tongues* and *peoples* would not be *standing before the throne, and before the Lamb, clothed with white robes, and palms in their hand, crying with a loud voice, Salvation to our God which sits upon the throne, and unto the Lamb.*[Re.7:9-10]

This prophecy is not yet fulfilled. **That is why we are soulwinners.**

God's No. 1 Job

That is one of the biblical reasons why we have sponsored so many thousands of national sons and daughters of the soil—national gospel ministers who have been enabled, with our assistance, to go and live among those *un*reached areas and tribes, as bonafide missionaries, and preach the gospel to them.

That is soulwinning. That is evangelism. That is what Christ authorized His followers to do. That is ministering life among the forgotten ones.

Christians talk about Christ's *second* coming. Millions have never heard of His *first* coming. They seek and receive *second* blessings while these forgotten ones have never experienced a *first* blessing. They pontificate about *re*fillings while multitudes have never experienced a *first* filling.

Should those on the front row receive a *second* serving of the Bread of Life while the hungry ones on the back rows have not yet received a *first* serving?

✧ ✧ ✧

WE HAVE DEDICATED our world ministry to the back rows, to the *un*churched, to the *un*saved, to the forgotten ones. This is the Christian's greatest mission in life. This guarantees success, happiness and fulfillment in ministry.

Once these forgotten ones have a chance to hear the gospel of Christ, Jesus will return as He said He would. That is why we are soulwinners— *Because Of The Unfulfilled Prophecies Concerning Christ's Return.*

SOULWINNING

Reason For Soulwinning

VI

THE
BLOOD OF
THE
*UN*CONVERTED

THERE ARE THOSE Christians who have God's vision—a world vision, a John 3:16 vision. They see Europe, Asia, Africa, North and South America, Australia, the Island nations—all the world, *every creature*. They have a trans-world vision.

Soulwinning is not reserved for missionaries, or preachers, or evangelists. You and I can do it. It is the priority in real Christianity, its heartbeat, its passion. ⬛➤

Chapter 15

Top Priority

W E ARE SOULWINNERS, *Because We Do Not Want The Blood Of The Unconverted On Our Hands.*

As a young Christian, one of the Bible portions which impressed me was in the third chapter of Ezekiel. God speaks about the reason that those who know Him should share His message with others—so that everyone can have a chance to receive His blessings.

I have made you a watcher...give warning from me. When I say to the wicked, you shall surely die; and you give no warning...to save lives; the wicked shall die in their iniquity; But their blood will I require at your hand.^{Ez.3:17-18}

Then later in the same book, God repeats that message: *If the watcher sees the sword coming, and does not blow the trumpet, and the people are not warned; if the sword comes and takes any person from among them, they are taken away in their iniquity;*

But their blood will I require at the watcher's hand.^{Ez.33:6}

In chapter thirty-three, the idea is stated again for additional emphasis. *When I say to the wicked, you shall surely die; if you do not speak to warn them from their way, the wicked shall die in their iniquity; but their blood will I require at your hand.*^{Ez.33:8}

Here are three witnesses to alert us that we can do something about the *unconverted* that will cause them to be saved instead of being lost.

Let's read some of these verses using contemporary terms to relate them to the soulwinner today:

I have made you a watcher. Therefore, hear the word at My mouth and give warning from Me. When I say to the unconverted, You shall surely die, and you give them no warning, nor speak to warn them of their ways, to save their lives; those same unconverted people shall die in their iniquities. But their blood will I require at your hand!

Yet if you warn the unconverted and they turn not from their sins, nor from their sinful ways, they shall die in their iniquities. But you have delivered your soul.

Motivation For Life

Their blood will I require at your hand. Each time Daisy and I read these words, we reviewed our priorities. Those Bible verses motivated us from the time we were teenagers. We did not, and I do not want the blood of the *un*converted required at our hands.

This is another reason we are soulwinners. This is why we share the gospel. This is why we have given, and continue to give, our lives to world-wide gospel ministry. This is why we have consistently done everything we could do, utilizing every tool for evangelism available to share Christ with the *un*reached. It is why we have sponsored so many thousands of national preachers as full time missionaries among the *un*churched peoples, tribes, villages and areas of the *un*evangelized world.

Literature In 132 Languages

This is why we have published many hundreds of tons of gospel literature in 132 languages and dialects; it is why we produce films and audio or video cassettes in around seventy major languages as tools for soulwinners and for release through mass media.

This is why we have witnessed the enormous growth of this world ministry. And this is why our daughter, Dr. LaDonna and I continue these mass crusades, national teaching seminars, and all of these evangelism outreaches around the world.

This is the reason for every outreach of this ministry, and why we encourage Christians to take part in the ministry of evangelism. By sharing in giving Christ's message to the world, they become soulwinners among the *un*reached as much as those who carry the message, and they share the rewards as much as those who share good news at the front.

We are people who have received word from the Lord, as Ezekiel talked about and our mission is to warn our world, like John the Baptist did, *to flee from the wrath to come.*[Mt.3:7]

In the words of the Apostle Paul: *Woe unto me if I do not preach the gospel.*[1Co.9:16] We do not want the blood of the *un*converted on our hands—either at home or abroad. So we choose to be soulwinners.

Lifetime Commitment

We do not pretend that we alone can win the world to Christ; but my daughter, Dr. LaDonna Osborn and I stay as involved in global evangelism as though God's plan depended upon us alone.

If we cannot win everyone, we can certainly win some—and we shall minister as though the reaping depended entirely on us.

A sophisticated businesswoman of prominence, who was touring our world headquarters in Tulsa, Oklahoma, requested an interview.

She was inquisitive and intelligent. We responded to her probing; then she gave us a final appraisal with these words: "Dr. Osborn, you seem to be very wrapped up in what you call world evangelism. Do you think that your activities alone will win the world to Christ?"

I responded, "No, but we intend to be involved as though the entire job depended on us."

She was pleased and became a partner in worldwide soulwinning.

We are soulwinners because we have taken God's word seriously. We do not want the blood of the *un*converted to be required at our hands. It is as simple as that!

Fastened to the east stone wall of the lobby of our world headquarters in Tulsa is a large metal sketch of the world. Adjacent to the map, in metal letters, are the words of our life's motto:

> *One Way-Jesus*
> *One Job-Evangelism*

The attention of all visitors is focused on this maxim to impress upon them the fact that this is a trans-world ministry. When God loved, He loved a world. When He gave His Son, He did it for a world. When Christ died, He died for a world. God's vision is a world vision. Our vision is too.

Measure The Vision

Many people are localized in their vision. They see *their* community. They think of *their* church or denomination but have little or no interest beyond those limits.

Others have a broader vision, spreading out to their state or province or tribe. They are concerned with evangelizing certain areas, but they have little concern beyond those borders.

Still others feel responsible for their nation. They will give and pray for the evangelization of their own country. But their vision is still localized. They are what we call *nationalistic* in their soulwinning interests.

There are others who have a broader vision that extends to the limits of their continent. They are interested in *continental* evangelism and will make any sacrifice to reach those boundaries. But even they are localized.

Getting God's Viewpoint

Then there are those Christians who have **God's vision — a world vision, a John 3:16 vision**. They see Europe, Asia, Africa, North and South America, Australia, the Island nations — all the world, *every creature*. They have a **trans-world vision**.

With jet aircraft, television, electronic mail and satellite communication, we live on a small crowded planet. The whole world is within our reach. So the Christian Church today can embrace a *world vision*.

Many times we have boarded a plane at some intercontinental airport abroad, soared off the runway, climbed to a great altitude, then looked back down upon the vast countryside.

I have often pondered the soulwinners we had encountered during our mission there. Before our arrival many of them only had a localized vision — limited by their cultural environment and by their religion.

They had not reached beyond the borders of their city or province or tribe or nation. Most of them had never traveled or had access to libraries or reading materials that might have expanded their thinking.

But in the course of our crusade and seminar, they had gotten God's viewpoint of their world. Their vision was no longer localized. They had become concerned for the whole of their globe.

As a result of seminars and conferences which we have conducted, we know of Africans engaged in evangelism in China; South Americans going to win souls in Alaska; Indonesians reaching the lost in Europe; Asians ministering in Caribbean nations; Filipinos proclaiming Christ in India; Koreans raising up churches in France; Brazilians carrying the gospel across Angola; and believers of other nations ministering around the world.

Probe The Priorities

Another vital phrase of our motto on the lobby wall of our world headquarters is:

Around the Clock—Around the World.

Most of our mass crusades and national seminars are conducted in countries abroad. Most of our literature is published in languages for the peoples of distant nations. Most of our world evangelism funds are used beyond our own homefront. Most of our evangelism projects concern reaching the *un*reached with the gospel. Most of our films, tapes, and other *Tools For Evangelism* are designed for soulwinning in other lands and for mass media abroad.

World evangelism is the top priority of this ministry. It is doing the thing that is nearest God's heart—the one thing Christ authorized every believer to do.

When it is top priority, one invests more in it than in anything else; one allots more time to it, more energy, more plans, more efforts, more thought, more money, more of life.

Taking personal action to share the gospel of Christ with all the world is the one way that we can make sure that the blood of the *unconverted* will not be required at our hands.

The Best Missionary Program

I lectured on *Giving For Missions* in a certain church. Afterwards, the pastor took me aside and said, "Dr. Osborn, I've been changed by listening to you today. I never perceived gospel missions abroad as a ministry potential for my own life. I expected that to be done by our missionaries, never realizing that I could personally be a gospel messenger abroad *without going overseas myself.* I never thought about investing to sponsor a *substitute* or to send printed or recorded preachers on my behalf."

Then he added, "I always had a great deal of pride in my denomination's missionary program. I believed that it was the best and I often spoke highly about it to others. It was not what *I* was doing, but what *my denomination* was doing, that made me proud. I talked about *our* organization, *our* program, *our* mission projects.

"But, Dr. Osborn, I personally invested very little in *our* missions program. If every member of my organization did like me, we would have no missionary programs. For me, it was a denominational project—not a personal involvement."

Soulwinning is not reserved for missionaries, or preachers, or evangelists. Soulwinning is the mission to which every Christian believer is called. You and I are the ones to whom this mission is committed. It is our priority, our life, our passion.

Too often Christians have been impressed that only professional clergy persons can serve as ministers. But Christ dwells in every believer. Each Christian is His witness. Every converted person becomes His mouthpiece. Christ wants to speak through believers. They are His witnesses. Millions of hurting, *un*loved, despairing people who would probably resist or resent the words of a clergy person will listen intently to an ordinary lay person who is willing to share what Christ has meant in his or her life.

The Portable Tool

An old man wept as he grasped my hand. Showing me his battered tape recorder, he said, "Dr. Osborn, you're my preacher. I carry you with me on tapes, from house to house, into hospitals, jails, and convalescent homes. I put you on that old machine and you preach for me. Then I pray for the listeners and they get saved and healed. I'm so glad that, at my advanced age, I can still be a soulwinner."

A Vision Is Born

SINCE OUR YOUTH, we have dreamed of ways to witness for Christ. Those dreams became visions. Visions inspired us to prayer. Faith put action to those prayers. Soon those dreams became living, pulsating realities.

Years ago, Daisy and I sat in Dr. Oswald J. Smith's missionary convention in Toronto, Canada, and dreamed of sending national foot-soldiers to the frontiers of evangelism, extending the gospel to *the regions beyond.*[2Co.10:16]

If people could have read our minds that day as we sat in *The People's Church*, they might have mocked us as youthful, emotional visionaries.

Other ministers listened to that tall, white-haired, aristocratic, missionary spokesman, Oswald J. Smith, as he shared the opportunity of world evangelism. They were impressed. They made notes on the statistics which he reported, but did little about it.

But that stately gentleman was building an unquenchable fire in the souls of Daisy and T.L. Osborn. A new vision was being conceived. Soon the program of *National Missionary Evangelism* was born and a new day dawned for sharing the gospel worldwide.

Pacesetters With Purpose

For more than half a century after that conference and that vision had been conceived in our young hearts, no Christian leader abroad ever had to say, "We would reach the *un*reached of our nation, but we don't have the funds."

We offered gospel leaders throughout the world regular monthly assistance for every trained, qualified national preacher, man or woman, whom they would send as full-time *missionaries* to the *un*reached.

Through that world-changing program, over 30,000 national preachers, male and female, have been sponsored as full-time *missionaries* in over 135,000 previously *un*reached tribes, towns, villages and areas that have, as a result, now received the gospel through these talented national messengers. This program has literally changed our world and has made it better.

The World's New Missionaries

FOR GENERATIONS, European and North American church denominations have been sending the gospel to the *non*-Christian nations of the world.

In almost every national crusade that we have ever conducted, in some eighty nations, our evangelism efforts have been culminated with a week-long seminar during which we teach several hours daily.

These periods of intense teaching have had national influence as we have emphasized that every Christian, whether male or female and of whatever tribe, color or race, is called and chosen by Christ to be His messenger.

Another truth which we have underscored in each nation is the fact that all believers of all nationalities are commissioned by our Lord to *go into all the world and preach the gospel to every creature.*[Mk.16:15] We have faithfully stressed that God never planned for the *whites* of Europe and North America to be His exclusive *Missionary Corps.* His plan is that each Christian of either sex and of any color or race should *go* with the gospel to the *unconverted.*

Diversity in *Missions*

During the earlier years of our world ministry, the term *missionary* only applied to light-skinned citizens of western, industrialized nations. Anointed Christian believers and leaders in the *third world* had never understood that they were qualified to be *missionaries.* That seemed both unreasonable and certainly unbiblical to us.

Everywhere we have ministered, we have emphasized that nationals can become the *best* missionaries because of advantages in language skills and in their familiarity with national living standards and cultural traditions.

Following our national crusades in Chile, we spent time with the pastors and gospel workers there, sharing with them the vision of world evangelism and the commission of Christ to reach *every creature.* No one had challenged them to reach the *un*reached of other nations. They responded without hesitation and began to take action.

As a result of those intense days of teaching, over thirty successful Chilean pastors took measures to install other ministers as pastors of their churches so that they could consecrate themselves and go as missionaries into the mountain areas of Argentina, Bolivia, Peru and into the Amazon jungles and delta areas of Brazil.

Some years later, a Chilean pastor wrote us from near the north pole. As a result of those world evangelism teaching sessions that we had conducted in Chile, he had gone as a *missionary* to minister among the Eskimos.

Christianity is no longer *headquartered* in Europe and North America. It has become nationalized worldwide. Already over half of the *missionaries* who are going *into all the world* are from nations traditionally regarded as *mission fields.* And their proportion is increasing every year.

From All Nations
To All Nations

A LEADING Christian periodical quotes recent findings of a coalition of mission groups. According to their report, the majority of Protestant missionaries throughout the world today are coming from *emerging* nations: 6,000 from India, 11,000 from other Asian nations, 8,000 from Latin American republics, and 15,000 from African countries are today serving as bonafide *missionaries*, promulgating the Christian gospel worldwide from nations that, until recently, were themselves called *mission fields*.

In recent decades, Mestizo Indians from the Amazon River basin have gone up the river and have established hundreds of new churches.

National *missionaries* from Korea are proclaiming Christ and are establishing churches and Bible Schools in over 70 different nations, and the Korean Church plans to have *missionaries* in every nation within a few more years.

Latin Americans are making significant inroads in Arabic nations. Their cultural values facilitate quicker relationships and better communication.

A theological seminary professor from Peru talks about the blossoming international movement of lay-missionaries—emerging world nationals who emigrate to other countries where they practice their professions, establish businesses or put down other economical roots in order to finance their real mission of communicating the gospel to the people. He says that from Peru alone, over 5,000 evangelicals believers emigrate to other nations annually whose faith and zeal motivates them to share the good news of Christ.

A Mighty Spiritual Force

A CHRISTIAN MAGAZINE reporter says, "Rather than being a clone of the *first* world Church, the *third* world Church is its alter ego. The Western Church is largely middle class, middle aged, and middle of the road. In contrast, the *third* world Church is considered to be poor in this world's goods, but unprejudiced, and spiritually alive. This makes for a spiritual force much more attuned to people coping with poverty, oppression, hunger, and whose traditions are more attuned to the supernatural."

An Argentinean leader speaks of "a mighty spiritual force" that is arising from among the "economically and politically weak *third* world." Specialists are talking of a "new era of Christianity, based in and emanating from the Southern continents," with teachings and methods that identify better with these societies.

New *Missions* Economics

Third world missionaries are sent out with little, if any money, and few tools. A South African church organization claims it can sponsor a *team* of workers for fifty American dollars a month and the clothes that they wear. One mission agency estimates that *third* world churches are funding several full time missionaries in foreign countries for what one Westernized missionary family may require.

A South American organization that has sent over 500 preachers and workers abroad from their country, as missionaries in other nations, insists that they live from the support that they receive in the nation where they minister. They believe that this policy motivates greater commitment to the task of evangelism and helps their missionaries to identify better with the problems of the people among whom they minister the gospel.

The high cost of Westernized missions, plus nationalistic attitudes, has greatly slowed the supply of *white* missionaries. International missiologists emphasize that this is not altogether negative. A specialist in church missions thinks the best way to reach the peoples of color is for them to see people of their own and other *third* world races preaching the gospel. This answers the nationalistic argument that "Christianity is the religion of the *whites*."

In free nations around the world, these changes are taking place as Christian leaders rediscover First Century soulwinning principles and God's value system that spans all races and both sexes.

National *Missions*—On The March

WHEN DAISY and I first went to Nigeria, a young pastor who had just left his job as a shoe salesman, chaired our crusade. He attended every session of our large teaching seminar that followed our mass crusade. We had loaded a 747 jet freighter with soulwinning tools and literature and had airlifted them into his nation, to be distributed at the end of our seminar.

That young pastor and his wife became aware of God's esteem for their lives. Their ministry became a dynamic example of leadership in their nation. Their spiritual fruit began to multiply until they built a cathedral that seats over twenty thousand people, plus raising up over 100 other churches in the city where they are headquartered.

In addition to that, over four thousand other new churches have been established across Nigeria under the anointed leadership of that couple. Their national membership has passed the *two million* mark, without counting the hundreds of churches and Bible schools that they have been instrumental in establishing in other African nations.

Nigeria is surrounded by French speaking nations. Since we speak French, we encouraged them to learn the language and to incorporate French classes in their international Bible school. Today they have graduated hundreds of young French speaking nationals from Zaire, Congo, Republic of Central Africa, Cameroon, Chad, Niger, Burkina-Fasso, Togo, Ivory Coast and other French speaking nations. Those graduates have now returned as *missionaries* to their homelands and are raising up new churches by the hundreds.

Thailand—Then And Now

When we first went to Thailand, there were less than a dozen Spirit-filled Christians in the whole nation, and most of them were Scandinavian missionaries. Today there are hundreds of strong churches established in Thailand, and Thai nationals have been commissioned and are serving as *missionaries* in many other nations.

The present superintendent of the largest Pentecostal organization in Thailand today, was a 14-year old lad when we conducted the first public, open air gospel crusade in Bangkok's history. He obtained permission from our residence hosts to sleep on his straw mat underneath the room where we stayed, because he believed that some of God's power would come upon him. In later years he became our interpreter, and today heads the fastest growing church organization in that Buddhist nation.

East Africa—Latin America

When we first went to East Africa, a lonely white missionary couple wanted us to help sponsor qualified nationals preachers so that they could devote their ministries to villages, tribes and areas *un*touched by the gospel.

Our historic crusade and teaching seminar there affected young men and women who came from all over Kenya. Today, that missionary couple reports that almost 4,000 new churches have been raised up as a result of our *National Missionary Assistance Program*. Today Kenyan nationals are serving as *missionaries* in many other African nations, and in other countries of the world.

For example, throughout the Caribbean and Central and South America, thousands of young men and women are today pastors, evangelists, establishers of Bible Schools, and leaders who attended one of our African crusades and followup teaching seminars in earlier years.

Women In God's Work

Today, women around the world are builders of churches and Bible Schools, they are pastors, missionaries, evangelists and leaders who have been inspired by the dynamic teaching and crusade ministries of my wife, Dr. Daisy and of our daughter, Dr. LaDonna Osborn. Their examples have effectively demonstrated a woman's identity, dignity, destiny and equality in God's redemptive plan. Daisy's five energizing books and LaDonna's revealing courses on *Redemption* are being used as textbooks worldwide, re-shaping the lives of women worldwide, motivating thousands of them to enter full time ministry.

Africa has been greatly affected by Dr. Daisy's *National Women's Congresses.* Hundreds of women are discovering themselves in the Bible through her teaching and that of Dr. LaDonna, her daughter, who was recently invited to Kenya by Archbishop Owiti, to officiate at the *first ordination service for women ever conducted in his nation.* Thousands of Kenyans attended the special event that was so large that it had to be celebrated at a public stadium.

Over 100 qualified, proven women were officially ordained for gospel ministry and were formerly presented certificates as members of the clergy. Most of them had already been in active ministry for years.

Some of these valiant women had instituted Bible schools, others had pioneered one or several churches, and some had successful evangelism ministries. But none of them had ever been officially recognized by the African Church or the government. Their public ordination was a significant forward step for the Church and for the nation.

One old village woman, over 70 years of age, was so inspired by what she learned and observed during Dr. Daisy's *National Women's Congress* that she resolved to dedicate the rest of her years to full time soulwinning ministry.

With her Bible and an old bicycle, within less than two years she had raised up seven new churches in seven villages and was pastoring them all, giving one day per week to each town church. She quipped: "If the good Lord had given us more days in a week, I could have established more churches."

In India, over 6,000 women attended Dr. Daisy's *National Congress for Women*. They came from many parts of India and from all levels of society; from government, from the academic, the medical and the business worlds, from villages and from cities. Nothing like it had ever been witnessed in India. Today hundreds of those Indian women are active in gospel ministries.

Gypsies To The Nations

When we first ministered in France, we shared in the great annual Gypsy Campmeetings. Thousands attended the crusade meetings at night and the teaching sessions during the day. We provided tons of our books and tracts, hundreds of tape players and thousands of our recorded gospel crusade messages in the French language.

Through our *National Missionary Assistance Program*, we sponsored a great number of those Gypsy preachers, through their organization, as full time *missionaries* in areas of Europe where the gospel had not been established. They began evangelizing and building churches all over France, Spain, Portugal, Italy, Greece and even parts of Germany and Austria. Today that Gypsy organization has spread the gospel all over Europe, in thousands of localities, and across India, South America, Eastern Europe and into other lands where they have located Gypsy populations.

We could report triumphs like these in many other areas like Taiwan, The Philippines, Holland, Germany, Indonesia, Papua New Guinea, India, in many nations of Africa, in Island nations, etc. *The world's new Missionary Corps is alive and on the march*, carrying out the commission of Jesus Christ to *preach the gospel to every creature.*

These are some of *the world's new missionaries* in action today.

Criticize Or Evangelize

THE STARTING POINT in soulwinning is to believe enough in the message of Christ to want to share it with others. That is what motivates one to think and to dream of ways to communicate the gospel and to win souls.

There are innumerable ideas for witnessing of Christ which any believer can implement. All thinkers are creators. All achievers in life are dreamers, thinkers, planners—and **doers**. Doers are often criticized.

Sooner or later, those who succeed in life learn that criticism is usually admiration awkwardly expressed. People often criticize the person who is out front. The unsuccessful, non-achieving person commands little attention and elicits no opposition.

Priority For Success

If we set high goals and achieve them, critics may ridicule us outwardly, but inwardly they will be challenged to become stronger and more daring themselves.

Criticism is a cheap commodity, always abundant, and certainly undeserving of our reaction. The person with *solutions* is the person in demand. Anyone can create problems, discuss them, analyze them, categorize them. Only the thinker—the creator, the achiever, the person of action—is the inventor of solutions.

Problems Or Solutions

Some of the best advice we ever read was a statement in *Reader's Digest*: "*Don't fight the problem; get on with the solution.*"

We have not spent our time holding conferences on how to win in evangelism. We have been getting on with the solution—spreading the gospel. We have not talked about the need for Christian literature. We have been supplying it.

We have not spent our time analyzing the problems of reaching the *un*reached. We have sponsored an army of gospel messengers and provided tons of soulwinning tools to augment the outreaches of tens of thousands of gospel messengers worldwide.

The enemies of the gospel have their eyes on the masses; *but we do too*, and we are doing something about it—something that works!

That is our policy: Action. Not conventions, not theories, not propositions, but action; not problems, but solutions; not questions, but answers.

It costs nothing to sit in group discussions, elaborating the problems of evangelism. But those with solutions pay dearly to communicate the good news to humankind. Solutions cost money. They cost lives. They demand dedication.

The millions of *un*reached tribal people in our world today are a problem. National evangelism is a solution that is working, so we get on with it.

Logical Tactics Applied

Our docu-miracle films are a solution. Millions are being reached through them. Other millions are being reached with our recorded audio and video gospel messages, mobile evangelism units, and the tons of our literature that we are constantly producing and shipping abroad for free distribution. Our choice is to stay engaged in providing solutions, not in analyzing problems.

While in Africa, a pastor there showed us a commercial company operating a fleet of fifteen beautiful four-wheel-drive vehicles equipped to show secular films. They constantly canvassed villages, gathered large crowds, showed their films, and advertised their products — beer, cigarettes, liquor, etc. which they marketed to the people. Missionaries had considered that those villages were not able to support a local church. But that secular company was having no problem reaping attractive financial profits.

Some church leaders in the area lamented: "What a reproach, that such products are being promoted in those villages. We must find a way to *stop those marketers*." They were obsessed by the problem and were doing nothing to provide a solution.

Daisy and I decided between ourselves: It will do no good to discuss with those church leaders this problem. We resolved to do something about it.

Another Vision Was Born

Our new trans-world, *Mobile Evangelism Program* was born. If business firms could prosper marketing secular products out in the villages of the world, the blessings of the gospel could be promulgated the same way. We began to provide completely equipped, four-wheel-drive mobile evangelism units for active soulwinning missions among the *un*reached.

We equipped each unit with a film projector and stand, a super-large rubber screen, a generator, a million dynamic gospel tracts and a set of our docu-miracle films in the local language.

Since then, we have shipped overseas more than a hundred large four-wheel-drive mobile units, equipped with every soulwinning tool that we produce in the language of the area.

The commercial world has been doing it. We are doing it too. The point is: we are not sitting and lamenting the spread of evil. We are *doing* something to spread the gospel.

Whose Opinion Counts Most?

A practical American president once said:

"It is not the critic who counts; not the one who points out how the strong one stumbled, or where the doer of deeds could have done better.

"The credit belongs to the one who is actually in the arena—in action—whose face may be marred by dust and sweat and blood, who may err and come short again and again; but who is spent in a worthy cause; who, if he fails, fails while daring greatly, but who has experienced the triumph of high achievement."

Yes, criticism and the inept persons who disseminate it, are plentiful. But solutions and the rare people who engender and apply them are rare and are valuable.

Critics come and go, rise and fall, appear and fade away; but problem-solvers are the pillars of society. It is not enough to bewail the decadence of this generation; you and I have the solution. We are Christian witnesses. We are soulwinners.

You can equip yourself with a supply of good gospel literature. Carry it with you wherever you go and sow the *good seed* in the lives of people wherever the occasion arises.

Acquire some good gospel audio cassettes or CDs. Invest in a player. Go out where the people are. Be a witness for Christ.

We are laborers together with God.[1 Co.3:9]

Seed As You Breed

After you discover the joy of soulwinning in your own community or area, perhaps you will want to provide some tools for soulwinners overseas. You can send audio cassette tapes or docu-miracle crusade videos in other languages to national Christian workers to use in evangelism in their nation. You will be involved in evangelism abroad and you will share the reward for the souls that are won this way, even though you may never go abroad yourself.

You can send literature for distribution in neglected villages. Don't wait for missionary organizations to do it. You are a Christian witness. You can do it.

Gospel messages on cassettes and CDs, or in books and tracts are always effective. They never tire or change their message or argue or compromise or become immoral. They communicate the same message to beggars as they do to royalty and patiently repeat their message as often as someone wants to listen. They are among the best gospel messengers in the world. And they will go as your substitutes.

It is not enough to just think or talk or pray about it. Success comes when action is coupled with convictions.

◇◇◇

WHEN YOU HAVE dedicated yourself to this top priority, then *if the unconverted turn not from their sinfulness, nor from their sinful ways, they shall die in their iniquities. But you will have delivered your soul.* Ez.3:19

That is the sixth reason we are soulwinners. *Because We Do Not Want The Blood Of The Unconverted On Our Hands.*

Reason For Soulwinning

VII

WHAT WE HAVE EXPERIENCED

AROUND THE WORLD, we have proven that people of all nations want to know the reality of God. But their spirits are never satisfied without knowing Christ. And without miracles, there was no way to prove that God is real, that Jesus Christ is presently alive and that the gospel is true today.

Ten thousand voices whirled over my head, saying, "You can do that. That is what Jesus did. That is what Peter and Paul did. That proves that the Bible way works today." The gospel, straightforward and in simple terms — not explained, but proclaimed — *is the power of God unto salvation to everyone who believes.*[Ro. 1:16] ⟾

Chapter 16

This Century

W E ARE SOULWINNERS, *Because Of What We Have Experienced.* During our mass evangelism crusades for over a half century in over eighty nations, the response has been the same.

Our most recent crusades have been the same as those conducted during our early ministry back in the forties and fifties—the same strategy, the same messages, the same hunger, the same multitudes, the same miracles, the same results.

Even though we human beings come and go, the gospel is the same in any generation when proclaimed in the power of the Holy Spirit.

Around the world, we have proven that people of all races, religions, and creeds want to know that God is real, that Jesus Christ is presently alive, and that the gospel is real today. Even with their many forms of worship, their superstitions and their religions, their spirits remain unsatisfied without Christ. They search for truth but are unable to find the peace they yearn for. They pray in many different ways, but do not receive answers. They seek God but do not experience Him in reality.

We have proven that once people are offered an opportunity to hear the gospel in simple language and *in demonstration of the Spirit and of power*,[1Co.2:4] they are eager to receive Jesus Christ.

In nation after nation, we have proclaimed Christ and His love. We never preach *against* superstitions or against other gods. We lift up Jesus Christ and His loving power. As people learn of Him and how to receive Him into their lives, they embrace Him and become His followers, abandoning superstitions and witchcraft.

Sometimes we have had to carry bags of charms and fetishes away from the campaign grounds and burn them, as Paul did.[Ac.19:18-19] When the people receive Christ, they no longer cling to fetishism and idolatry; they no longer trust in graven images for protection from evil spirits. *JESUS* is enough.

Our Dilemma Among Eastern Religions

Daisy and I went to India when we were only twenty and twenty-one years of age. We did not comprehend the miracle part of Christ's commission. He had said to *go into all the world*[Mk.16:15] and we had obeyed. But His words, *these signs shall follow them that believe*, etc., were beyond our grasp since we had not yet learned that miracle faith is simply acting on God's word of promise.

Supernatural confirmation of our preaching was not witnessed. We led a few souls to Christ, but for the most part our mission was a disheartening experience for us.

When we preached or taught about Jesus Christ, Hindus kindly accepted Him in theory as another good god to worship *along with their other deities*—but no change resulted in their lives.

Moslems reasoned: "How do you know that Jesus Christ is God's Son or that He was raised from the dead?" They believed that He was a good man, even a prophet with some healing power, but not that He is the savior of the world, that His blood was divine—and certainly not that He is risen from the dead.

We did our best to convince them that Jesus Christ is God's Son, and that He shed His blood, and died for the salvation of everyone who would believe in Him.

"Can you prove those things?" they asked.

"Yes we can. Look at these Bible verses," we said. "Listen to what they say."

"What is that book that you are reading from?" they asked. "The Bible, God's holy word!" we replied.

"Oh, no," they retorted, "That is not God's word. *This* is God's word!" And they showed us their *Koran*.

"What is *that*?" I asked? "It is the *Koran*, the holy word of God as given through His holy prophet Mohammed!" they responded.

"No!" I said. "*That* is not God's word. *This* is God's word!" I insisted, indicating my Bible.

Who was right? Which holy book contained God's message? The *Bible* or the *Koran*? How could we know? What was the proof? Both were beautiful books. Both were bound in black leather with golden titles embossed on their covers.

Preaching Without Proof

Without miracles, there was no way that we could prove to them that the Bible is God's word. We felt helpless, incompetent and embarrassed.

Facing that dilemma, we made a wise decision. We returned to our country, demoralized, discouraged and broken in spirit.

But we had seen the masses of the beautiful peoples in India, and we never stopped in our search for the solution to our problem until we had found God's answer.

We fasted and prayed. We could not forget those underprivileged millions. They needed Christ. We desired to win them. We felt compelled in our spirits to find the answer?

God saw our bewilderment and began the process of revealing to us His solution to human need. We heard a remarkable woman of God, Rev. Hattie Hammond, preach a great message at the Assemblies of God campmeeting in Brooks, Oregon. Her theme: *If you ever see Jesus, you can never be the same again.*

Daisy and I wept as we listened. We drove home to McMinnville, Oregon where we were pastoring a wonderful church, wiping tears to see the road.

Jesus Appeared

The next morning at six o'clock, Jesus Christ walked into our bedroom. When I saw Him, it seemed as though all physical strength left my body. I lay there as though paralyzed, unable to move a finger or a toe. Water poured from my eyes, though I was not conscious of weeping.

I do not know how long I gazed into His penetrating eyes before He faded from my sight, nor how long it was before I could move from my bed onto the floor where I lay before Him, face down, until the afternoon.

When I walked out of our room that day, I was a new man. *I had beheld my Master*. He did not represent a religion. He was *Life!* He was real. He became the Lord of my life that day in a way I had not known Him before.

My attitude toward life and toward the ministry was transformed. Denominational leaders would no longer be the primary influence in my life. Aspiration to influence in our denomination was gone. *The passion of my life was to please Jesus and to do His bidding.*

Following that experience, a man of God came to our city, preaching and ministering to the sick. We witnessed hundreds of conversions and instant miracles of healing.

As we sat in that auditorium watching Christ minister through that humble man, ten thousand voices whirled over my head, saying, *"You can do that. That's what Jesus did. That's what Peter and Paul did. That proves that the Bible way works today. You can do that because that's the way they did it in the Bible."*

Jamaica, Puerto Rico, Haiti, Cuba

WE TURNED once again to the *unreached* peoples of our world. We began in Jamaica. In thirteen weeks over nine thousand souls accepted

Christ. Ninety totally blind people were healed. One hundred and twenty-five deaf mutes were restored. Many hundreds of other miracles took place as the *Lord worked with us, confirming His word with signs following.*[Mk.16:20]

Next, we went to Puerto Rico. The crusades there were massive. Our message was simple. The people wanted reality. They believed on Christ and embraced Him as their savior when *they saw His miracles which he did on them that were diseased.*[Jn.6:2]

Our next crusade was in Haiti where the same results were repeated again. Throngs too large for any building filled the big compound and the adjacent roadway as we *gave witness of the resurrection of the Lord Jesus: and great grace was upon us.*[Ac.4:33]

After those triumphs in Jamaica and Puerto Rico, we went to Cuba. By that time, it began to look like more than just a spontaneous spiritual visitation in a couple of countries. It was clearly a pattern—a biblical pattern.

The Caribbean Challenge

These historic mass crusades in the Caribbean area were being heralded across the world.

But tradition in the church is strong, and sometimes unrelenting. Well-meaning ministers began to console us and to prepare us for inevitable failure. We were told that we must not expect such things to happen everywhere we would go.

Some counseled us that God may show His power in a certain area, for a particular reason, but that we should not expect similar results in other nations.

We were told to expect defeats as well as successes; that this is how God keeps us from spiritual pride that would eventually thwart our usefulness in His service.

All of this sounded traditionally pessimistic to us. We continued believing that the Lord would confirm the gospel wherever we proclaimed it. We were convinced that the great commission which Jesus gave was for *every nation*, and for *every creature*. He promised confirmation *unto the end of the world*, and He did not mention any exceptions.

We believed that any people of any nation in the whole world would believe the gospel message if they could have the opportunity to see it confirmed by signs, wonders and miracles.

We were not prepared for failures then, and we never have been. We believe in success. Christ does not fail. He is faithful to confirm His word. The gospel cannot fail.

When we arrived in Cuba, spiritual leaders counseled us about the wisdom of balance and patience, that we should not necessarily expect great crowds in Cuba just because of the successes we had experienced elsewhere.

Their logic asserted that, "Jamaica was traditionally Christian already; that Puerto Rico, of course, was so influenced by the United States that religious opposition was not a factor there; that in Haiti, the cultural traditions of the people had always influenced a strong tendency toward spiritism."

"But here in Cuba," they solemnly counseled us, "the people are staunchly devoted to their traditional religion and we should not anticipate the same results."

Despite such negativism, the Cuban people were just as responsive as those of the other nations where we had been.

There was tough religious opposition, but it only tended to promote our meetings. An organized procession of one hundred religious leaders marched in the streets to dissuade the public from attending our mass crusade, but many thousands came and turned to the Lord.

Victory in Latin America

OUR NEXT MISSION was Venezuela. I still remember the counsel we received there: "T.L. and Daisy, it's different here. In Cuba and in Puerto Rico, religious opposition is mild because the people are influenced by the United States. But here you are on the South American continent. You could be arrested and incarcerated, or even stoned."

But ministry in beautiful Venezuela was exactly like it had been in lovely Jamaica, in dynamic Puerto Rico, in responsive Haiti, and in wonderful Cuba. Multitudes believed on Christ and received Him into their hearts as they witnessed the miraculous confirmation of the gospel. The people of Venezuela were no different.

From Venezuela we went to Asuncion, Paraguay where thousands jammed the big ball field on the opening night. The results would have been the same as in other nations but religious opposition was raised and the authorities refused to allow the meetings to continue.

So we proceeded to Santiago de Chile where we preached to multitudes at the national stadium for four weeks and terminated the crusade with a parade of people, who had been healed, that was so long that it took over an hour to pass a single point.

Jubilation In Japan

THEN WE TRAVELED to Japan. When word was received that we were contemplating crusades there, letters were rushed to us: "Don't come here. Japan is difficult. Miracles are not for this nation. The Japanese people are only interested in academic enlightenment. They look to their ancestors as their spiritual source.

Nervous church leaders were apprehensive about us expecting miracles to confirm our preaching in Japan. They argued: "There are many healing cults among the Japanese people. Christians here do not want to be identified with these superstitions. Besides, miracles will never convince the Japanese people about Jesus Christ."

Others said, "Japan is Buddhist and Shintoist. People in the western hemisphere are easy to reach. They already believe the Bible. They believe that Jesus is God's Son and that His blood was shed for our sins. But the Japanese would never believe this. You won't find it the same here. These people are not emotional. We can only appeal to them on intellectual and academic levels."

The pattern of success in our crusades seemed to pose a threat to predominant Japanese church traditions.

At that time, it was unheard of to go to a *non-*Christian nation, to preach out in open public places, and to reap thousands of souls for Christ. Some contended that our success was the result of emotionalism, that the converts of this *new mass evangelism hysteria* could not be authentic and would not endure.

Missionaries and church leaders had not done things that way. They had labored patiently for years. Although they may not have won so many converts, those they had won were *solid and genuine*. Those who claimed to receive Christ in the Osborn-style meetings could not be transformed people. These so called converts would not endure.

Daisy and I had heard all of this in India when we had been young missionaries, unable to win people to the Lord. Senior missionaries there had tried to impress us that we should not expect to convince people about Jesus. One of them had told us: "I've been a missionary here for five years and have never won a Hindu to Christ. That's the way it is in India. You must learn patience." We left India because we refused to succumb to that kind of negativism.

Now, the years had passed and we had proven the power of the gospel in many lands. But in Japan, we were once again confronted by the same pessimism that had caused us to leave India. Our evangelism success seemed to pose a threat instead of a blessing. Established missionary thinking was discounting anything that might precipitate change in instituted policies.

Buddhists And Shintoists

But God wanted to show His people *everywhere* that there are no exceptions in gospel evangelism, that His great commission would prove effective *wherever* the gospel would be proclaimed with living faith and action.

Not all church leaders in Japan were pessimistic. Some wrote, "Come and help us too. Modernism can never save the Japanese. They must see miracles and we believe that they will respond positively to the gospel when they see it confirmed by signs and miracles!"

I still recall the logic of a Baptist pastor who wrote: "Japan is full of phony healing cults. The Japanese must see the real thing. Our modern churches lack miracle power. Come and help us. You have what we need to win this vast nation for Christ."

We accepted their challenge and Japan proved to be just like Jamaica, Puerto Rico, Haiti, Cuba, and the nations of South and Central America. When they saw the miracles, the beautiful Japanese people screamed, wept, and repented with as much, or more emotion than we had seen in other nations.

We went to the religious heart of historic Japan—the famous ancient city of Kyoto. There on a large field not far from the enormous Shintoist temples of the city, thousands of enthusiastic Japanese people were spellbound by the gospel message of Christ. Forty-four deaf mutes claimed healing during that three-week crusade.

Many remarkable miracles were wrought in Kyoto. Blind people were healed. Paralyzed and crippled people walked again. Those with incurable diseases, with fevers and other painful infirmities were made whole. God confirmed his word in miraculous ways to show the Japanese people how He loves them and wants to bless them

Then we followed with other wonderful crusades in the cities of Nagoya and Matsuyama. In each crusade, the results were the same.

Those Shintoists and Buddhists acted just like the peoples of the Caribbean area or of Latin America. Thousands believed on Christ.

Triumph In Thailand

ONE OF OUR next missions was to Thailand—the strong Buddhist monarchy of Southeast Asia. Again we were advised: "This won't be like Japan. The Japanese Buddhists have been influenced by the post-war occupation of the Americans. They are responsive to western ideas. But here in Thailand, ancient Buddhism is intrinsically woven into the social fabric of Thai culture and religion. They have never been ruled by a foreign power and are indifferent to the ideas of Western religions."

When we first ministered to those stoic Thai people, there were less than a dozen people in the entire country who had received an apostolic baptism of the Holy Spirit—and they were mostly Scandinavian missionaries. And even most of them (with the notable exception of one couple) were hesitant about the idea of proclaiming the gospel out in public places. It was felt that this would violate Thai culture.

Being such a serene and sensitive people, a public crusade like we proposed would be too aggressive. It was felt that any gospel approach in Thailand must be in keeping with their traditional poise and reserved stoicism.

I am thankful that I can report that when the Thai people witnessed blind people receiving their sight, cripples walking, lepers being cleansed, and the deaf hearing again, their response was no different than it had been among the Jamaicans, the Puerto Ricans, the Haitians, the Cubans, the Latin Americans—or the Japanese. *They believed the gospel when they saw it confirmed by miracles, and they received Christ into their hearts and began to follow Him exactly as people were doing in other nations.*

Today, there are thousands of Spirit-filled Christians all over Thailand. Great soulwinning ministries are flourishing there. National pastors are building strong and vibrant churches that are now spreading the gospel in other nations of that burgeoning part of the world.

Islamic Indonesia

AFTER THIS, our next challenge was Indonesia, a nation that was ninety-five percent Moslem at that time.

Around the world we had heard how difficult it was to persuade Islamic people to believe the gospel and to embrace Jesus Christ as savior. The helplessness we had experienced in India where we had first gone as missionaries, almost haunted us. But by the time we reached Jakarta, the capital city of Indonesia, things were different. We had learned to proclaim the gospel with apostolic confirmation of signs, miracles, and wonders. We firmly believed that Indonesia would be no different than other nations had been.

The first night of our evangelism crusade in Jakarta, we estimated that around 40,000 people had converged on the great field to hear what we had to say. After completing that first message about Jesus, I was impressed to do something quite unusual.

I told them that I did not expect them to make a decision about Jesus Christ until He proved Himself to be alive by undeniable miracles. I expressed our feelings that a dead Christ could do them no good.

I emphasized the fact that Jesus Christ was confirmed by miracles two thousand years ago; Ac.2:22 and that if He is alive today, then God would confirm this fact by doing miracles like those He performed before He was crucified.

I knew that Moslems are aware of the existence of a historical figure known as Jesus of Nazareth. They know that He was a good man, even a prophet with healing powers. They are aware that He was crucified. But they are persuaded that the Christian teaching of His resurrection and of His blood being shed for the remission of the sins of the world is unfounded.

We learned during that great crusade in Jakarta that there is only one way to convince the Moslem world about Christ. If Jesus is alive, let Him do the miracles which He did before He was killed. If He is dead, He cannot. If He is risen and unchanged today, He will.

I offered to pray for those who were deaf in the audience. I explained that I would pray *in Jesus' name*. If Christ is dead, His name would have no power. If He is alive, He would do what He did in Bible days.

The Moslem Hadji

The first person to come to the platform for prayer was a Moslem *hadji* about fifty-five years old, wearing a black fez which indicated that he had been a pilgrim to the venerated Islamic city of Mecca in Saudi Arabia.

He had been born totally deaf in one of his ears. He explained that he had never heard a sound in that ear.

I carefully witnessed to him about Jesus Christ, then told him how I would pray. I explained that God was looking down upon us. I witnessed to him that God had raised Jesus, His Son, from the dead. I explained that God wanted people to know that Christ is alive and that He would therefore, confirm that He had raised His Son from the dead. I emphasized to the man, and to the multitude, that God would give evidence of these biblical facts by miraculously opening this ear that had never heard a sound.

Then I said to the audience: "If this man does not hear when I have prayed for him in the name of Jesus, you can say that we are false witnesses of Jesus Christ and that He is not risen from the dead. But if God does answer our prayer and create hearing in this man's ear, then you will know that Christ is alive, because a dead Christ cannot do such a miracle."

I looked at that Moslem teacher, then made another strange decision. I decided *not even to pray for his healing*, but to just *speak* in the authority of Christ. Neither did I ask the people to bow their heads or to close their eyes. I wanted them to *see* everything that I did. Furthermore, I decided not to even touch his deaf ear with my hand because I wanted the people to know that there was no magical power or mystical touch involved.

I spoke these words with calmness and authority: *"That it may be known that Jesus Christ is God's Son, risen from the dead according to the scriptures, and that only through His blood can anyone be saved; give life to this deaf ear so it can hear—in Jesus' name!"*

Missions With Miracles

The entire audience gasped when that hadji could hear the faintest whisper and even the ticking of my wife's tiny mechanical wrist watch.

Thousands raised their hands that night indicating that they were convinced that Jesus Christ is alive and that they wanted to receive Him as their savior. How different this was from the embarrassment that we had suffered several years earlier in trying to convince Moslems and Hindus in India about Christ

The Indonesians responded exactly like the Japanese did when they saw miraculous proof of the gospel of Jesus Christ. *If we take miracles out of Christianity, then about all that we have left is another ceremonial religion.*

The Islamic people know that their prophet, *Mohammed, is dead.* Christian believers know that our prophet, *Jesus, is alive.* When that is proven by miracles, it has been my experience that people of other religions no longer adhere to their former beliefs but become eager followers of Christ who gives proof that He is risen from the dead.

This is why Jesus commissioned His followers to *preach the gospel to every creature,*[Mk.16:15] promising that supernatural signs would *follow them that believe*[Mk.16:17] — *among all nations,*[Mt.28:19] *unto the end of the world.*[Mt.28:20] He knew that miracles would always be necessary for the world to know that He is alive.

When we had been in India as young missionaries, we were challenged: "Prove that your Christ lives!" We were unable to respond. So we opted to leave India rather than to acquiesce to the *status quo* that seemed to us to engender little more than slow but sure spiritual stagnation, without the joy of bearing fruit in our ministry. But now in Indonesia, *we* were different. *We* had been transformed. *We* had proven that the living Christ wants to give proof of His word.

The Angry Moslem Zealot

One evening in that pace-setting Jakarta crusade, a young fanatical Moslem teacher pressed through the crowd toward the platform to interrupt my preaching. Daisy spotted him coming and intercepted him at the steps.

He asserted, "That man is a false teacher. Jesus is dead. He is not God's Son. Let me speak to our people about Mohammed, God's true prophet." Daisy tried to reason with him, but he was too emotional.

Finally, she told the young zealot: "Listen, I'm a Christian lady and here's what I am willing to do. I will interrupt my husband on one condition: You and I will go together to the microphone. We will not argue. We will see whether Mohammed or Jesus is the true prophet of God and the savior of the world.

"We will call for someone totally blind to come forward. You pray for that person, in the presence of the people and in the name of Mohammed. If sight is restored by a miracle, we will reappraise our attitude about your religion.

"If no miracle takes place, then as a believing Christian woman, I will pray for that person in the name of Jesus Christ. If sight is miraculously restored, then your people will know that what the Bible says about Christ is true."

The young Moslem turned in a rage and disappeared in the crowd. This was what we had not been able to do in India as young missionaries.

Return To India

AFTER OUR ENORMOUS crusades in Java, we finally experienced the joy of returning to India, fourteen years after we had been unsuccessful in witnessing for Christ there. We went back to the same university city of Lucknow where we had been unable to demonstrate to the people that Jesus Christ is the living, resurrected Son of God and savior of the world.

This time, things were different because WE were different. Multitudes of from fifty to seventy-five thousand people converged on a big field adjacent to the provincial stadium grounds.

We preached that *Jesus Christ is the same yesterday, today and forever.*[He.13:8] Then we prayed for that multitude of people. The gospel we had proclaimed to them was mightily confirmed by our Lord. The deaf heard. Cripples walked. Blind people received their sight. Lepers were cleansed. And thousands believed on Christ and accepted

Him as their Lord. We were truly reliving Bible days.

Jesus showed Himself alive in India. Our search for truth had paid off. This was apostolic, biblical evangelism in action in our generation.

Christ showed [and continues to show] *himself alive by many infallible proofs.*Ac.1:3

Christ Visits A Hindu

A young Hindu university student stood amidst the multitude there in Lucknow, ridiculing everything that we said or did. He was a member of a radical Hindu group that had vowed to drive Christianity from the shores of India.

When we prayed for the people that night, Jesus Christ, dressed in a purple robe, suddenly appeared to that young extremist. The Lord opened his nail-pierced hands and extended them to the young man, speaking these words: *"Behold my hands, I am Jesus."*

The man fell to the ground, weeping, repenting, sobbing. Then he pushed his way through the mass of people, to the platform, where he took the microphone in his trembling hands and, with tears bathing his face, told that multitude what he had seen. He urged his people to believe on Jesus, and thousands of them did.

How different our crusade was than our little meetings had been in that city, fourteen years earlier! With miraculous confirmation of the gospel, India proved to be no different than Jamaica, or Puerto Rico, or Haiti, or Cuba, or Latin America, or Japan, or Thailand, or Indonesia — or other nations where we had already ministered the gospel.

Miracles In Africa

THEN, IT WAS AFRICA. Again, we witnessed enormous crusades — the first mass miracle evangelism crusades ever to be celebrated across that vast continent. Again, the evidence was clear that people are the same everywhere.

A noted beggar, a devout Moslem, had been paralyzed by polio when he was a child and had crawled on the ground for thirty years. He dragged himself along the dusty roadway to the racetrack where we were conducting our crusade.

The beggar listened to the gospel and as he believed on Jesus Christ, he was instantly healed. He pushed through the crowd and stood before the multitude of 80,000 people to give witness of the mighty miracle that he had received.

As he stood there weeping, he cried out: "Jesus Christ must be alive! Otherwise, how could He have healed me? Mohammed is dead, but Jesus lives. Look at me. You know me. I have begged in your streets. Now I can walk. Look! This Jesus lives!"

What that Moslem beggar expressed was the greatest message that could be proclaimed about the risen Christ. It sounded like a miracle testimony from the book of Acts.

Jesus For A Hurting World

Around the world we have seen that people want Christ *when they see evidence that He is the same today as He was in Bible days.* They are ready to believe when there is proof that He lives.

God made all human beings alike. *He has made of one blood all nations of people for to dwell on all the face of the earth.*[Ac.17:26] People are made to walk with God. They instinctively seek Him. This is why every *un*evangelized tribe or people on earth practices some kind of religious ritual or ceremony in their desperate search for a living God.

The gospel, presented direct and in simple terms—not explained, but proclaimed—reveals this Living Christ. It *is the power of God unto salvation to everyone who believes.*[Ro. 1:16]

People want to know the true and living God. Our task is to preach the gospel, to witness of Christ, to tell of Him and to confess Him everywhere—to crowds or to individuals, in public places or in private homes. People want what Bible believing Christians have. We have proven this worldwide. *This is why we are soulwinners.*

Europe's Response

THE CYNIC MAY argue, "What you report may be true among the peoples of emerging nations, but it is not true in the modern, industrialized world!"

But the fact is that one of our greatest crusades, where audiences numbered over a hundred thousand people nightly, was in the capital city of orthodox, traditional, Christian Holland — The Hague.

When sophisticated Europe witnessed the miracles of Christ as He faithfully confirmed His word with signs and wonders in our crusades here, multiplied thousands of Hollanders and of other Europeans received the Lord for the first time in their lives.

The results have proven to be the same wherever we have proclaimed the gospel, either in large auditoriums, out on open fields, or under the canopies of huge tents, all over Europe, Great Britain and North America.

Ex-Soviet Union & China

Recently we ministered in the ten largest cities of the ex-Soviet Union including Moscow, the capitals of Kazakhstan, Kirghizstan, the Ukraine, Lithuania, Siberia, and Belarus. Then we ministered in the four largest cities of Poland, and we are now planning crusades in Bulgaria, Hungary and again in the Ukraine.

In every city where we have gone, the large auditoriums that we have used have been packed with thousands of people eager to know about God, about Jesus and about the miracle gospel. *In each crusade or conference, God has confirmed His word exactly the same as He has done in nations and cities around the world.* In every city, we have seeded the people for *Soulwinning*, and have given each adult a copy of this, and of nine of our other major books.

We have set our sights on the other nations of East Europe, on the Moslem world and on China. Our major books are translated and published in Bulgarian, Hungarian, Russian, Polish, Lithuanian and they are being prepared for publication in other East European nations. They are already published in the principal Chinese language of Mandarin and are being carried secretly to over 8,000 underground preaching points across that vast nation. We are seeding the peoples of those countries for *Soulwinning*—the work and ministry nearest the heart of God.

As Paul said: *There is no difference...for the same Lord over all is rich unto all that call upon him.*[Ro.10:12]

Outbreak In Soulwinning

We first published these *Seven Reasons Why We Are Soulwinners* in our magazine *Faith Digest* which we mailed monthly, and free, to hundreds of thousands of Christians and gospel ministers in well over a hundred nations.

From around the world, letters poured into our offices acclaiming this series of articles as among the most challenging material on soulwinning that they had read. As a result, hundreds of believers, preachers, missionaries and national leaders have recommitted themselves to minister to the *un*converted with a fresh passion.

Tens of thousands of Christians are taking gospel literature, anointed messages on cassettes, and other soulwinning tools out into market places, streets, homes, jails, hospitals, etc. They are active in face to face evangelism, praying for the sick and leading the *un*converted to Christ— *out where the people are!*

This is what the First Century Church did and this is what is happening again in this century— among those who really believe what is recorded in the Gospels and in the Acts of the Apostles. This is what we are encouraging believers to do around the world. This is why we have edited, revised and enlarged this book on *Soulwinning*. The material it contains is producing fresh motivation in the lives of thousands of Christians worldwide.

When we first published this book, we sent gift-copies to more than 125,000 pastors, missionaries, preachers and national leaders worldwide as our investment to motivate an international renaissance of the biblical evangelism.

Then we wrote the sequel to this book under the title, *Outside The Sanctuary*, which we also circulated worldwide. (Later we combined the two books into this one enlarged and revised edition of *Soulwinning*).

Sharing this vision on a world scale has motivated thousands of anointed and committed men and women to launch all kinds of soulwinning programs. Their leadership has resulted in the reaching of multiplied millions of *un*reached, *un*converted and neglected people with the message of Christ who had never received the gospel.

Because we know that people want Christ, and because we have proven that fact worldwide, *we are soulwinners*.

◇ ◇ ◇

SHARING CHRIST WITH people is the greatest opportunity on earth for believing Christians. Many soulwinning organizations today offer evangelism tools and literature that are dynamic and powerful. They are available to you, so let them open the door to fresh new ministries of reaching people with the gospel witness of Christ—not only in your own area but everywhere that new possibilities arise.

That is the seventh reason we are soulwinners:—*Because Of What We Have Experienced.*

T.L. and Daisy Osborn have been teammates in evangelism for over half a century, proclaiming the gospel of Christ and sharing His love with millions of people, face to face, in more than 70 nations. Here they rejoice together on the final day of another triumphant soulwinning crusade.

"We're bringing hope and faith to tens of thousands who have known nothing but Godless communism."

Osborn brings miracle life to thousands of Ukrainians.

T.L. & LaDonna are giving their BEST to reach nations with the gospel—often on *two fronts at once.*

T.L. Osborn proclaims the gospel to thousands in Lithuania where communism dominated since Lenin's Godless revolution. Today the new church is on the rise.

Dr. T.L. and Bishop LaDonna Osborn minister across ten major cities of the ex-Soviet Union, proclaiming the miracle-producing gospel to packed auditoriums in every city, and giving a full set of Osborns' 10 books to each adult.

Dr. LaDonna in Beijing, dedicates tons of T.L.'s book, *"Healing the Sick"*, in Mandarin Chinese language.

One fifth of the world lives in China. *"Why should anyone hear the gospel twice before everyone has heard it once?"* We are seeding China NOW.

医治
疾病

Osborn books in Mandarin, seeding for China's great soul harvest.

China has influenced the world for over 5,000 years. Now, the *old* is giving way to the *new*. God's LOVE and redemptive plan for humanity is the only hope for these millions.

Kharkov, Ukraine auditorium is packed for Osborns' Ministry.

LaDonna shocks Kharkov with her dynamic preaching. Seeing her preach with power, then pray with faith, and seeing miracles manifested, is evidence to these tough people that God does not limit women in ministry.

The Osborns' books and tracts are published in 132 languages, (their docu-miracle crusade films, videos and audio cassettes in 67 languages). These are scattered throughout the world, and are among the most effective Tools for Evangelism known, communicating the gospel to millions of people.

OSBORN CRUSADE — Uyo

OSBORN CRUSADE — Kinshasa

OSBORN CRUSADE — W. Africa

OSBORN CRUSADE — Calabar

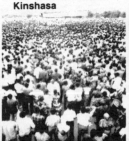

cassettes, in 67 languages, witness to millions of souls worldwide.

Largest Soulwinning Seminar in Kenya's history, conducted by the

Above: Tons of Osborns' Soulwinning Tools for African church leaders.

Osborns. 5,000 national church leaders attend from seven nations.

Below: The Osborn Soulwinning Seminar, under big Bamboo Cathedral.

"TALKING BOX" shares the big love-plan with New Guinea man in his own dialect. T.L. assures him that God is saying, "I love you. I value you. I created you for my BEST."

Love does not see traditional and cultural barriers. Love sees the person of this Pokot tribeswoman with whom Daisy shares the message of Christ.

The Osborn gospel literature is published in 132 languages. Here Christian workers in Thailand unload a large shipment for soulwinning outreaches there.

The Osborns conduct Evangelism Seminars for Christian workers around the world, like this one in the capitol city of Bangkok, Thailand. (Photos — Top: United in prayer after a strategic teaching session. Bottom: Posing for photograph on the final day of the seminar. Center and opposite page: Equipped for soulwinning outreaches nationwide.

WOMEN'S NATIONAL CONFERENCE — E. AFRICA

Daisy Osborn seeds the women of the world in her national women's mass rallies abroad.

INDONESIAN WOMEN'S DAY — SURABAJA

WOMEN'S NATIONAL MIRACLE DAY — KAMPALA

AUSTRALIAN CONFERENCE

Daisy proclaims the gospel at Municipal Stadium in Surabaya, Java, (Below) Osborn daughter, LaDonna, pastor of International Gospel Center at Tulsa, OK, preaches Christ at stadium in Papua New Guinea.

Following their triumphant crusade in West Africa, the Osborns airlift tons of Tools for Evangelism into the nation to equip thousands of national preachers to reach the lost.

Dedicating another airlift of Soulwinning Tools for national preachers and workers in Papua New Guinea.

T.L. AND DAISY OSBORN CRUSADES WORLDWIDE. For over half a century, in 73 nations, they have been pace-setters in mass-evangelism. It is believed that they have shared Christ with more non-Christians, face to face, than any couple who has ever lived.

CARIBBEAN — Ponce, Puerto Rico

AFRICA — Kinshas, Zaire

INDONESIA — Surabaya, Java

MEXICO — Monterrey

PHILIPPINES — Cabanatuan

T.L. AND DAISY
OSBORN
MASS EVANGELISM
CRUSADES (Cont'd)

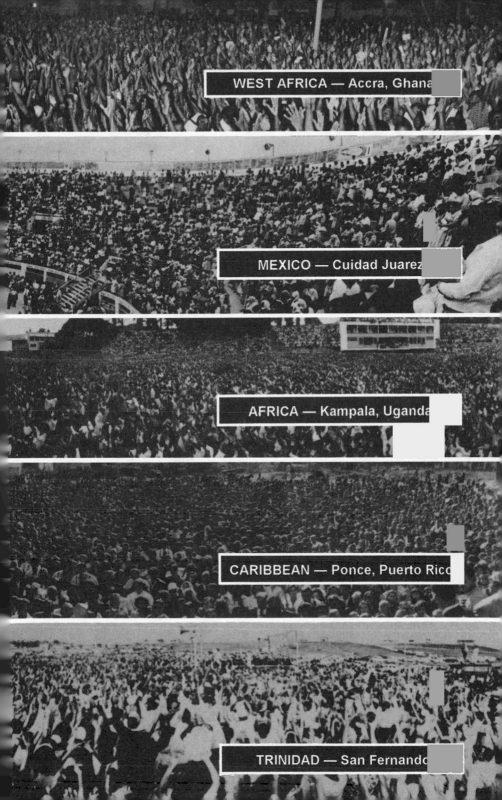

WEST AFRICA — Accra, Ghana

MEXICO — Cuidad Juarez

AFRICA — Kampala, Uganda

CARIBBEAN — Ponce, Puerto Rico

TRINIDAD — San Fernando

T.L. AND DAISY
OSBORN
MASS EVANGELISM
CRUSADES (Cont'd)

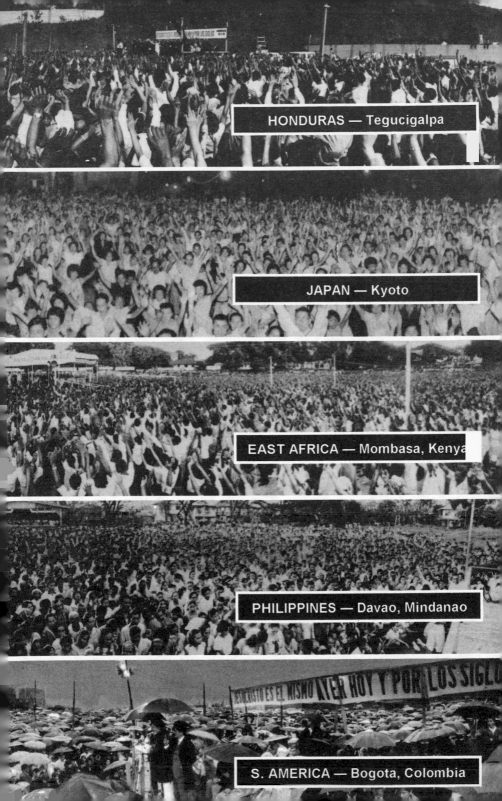

HONDURAS — Tegucigalpa

JAPAN — Kyoto

EAST AFRICA — Mombasa, Kenya

PHILIPPINES — Davao, Mindanao

S. AMERICA — Bogota, Colombia

SUPERIMPOSED PHOTOGRAPH

Both T.L. and Daisy Osborn believe and proclaim that "The preaching of the cross ... is the power of God;" that "The Gospel is the power of God unto salvation to every-one that believes." They contend that no one has the right to hear the Good News repeatedly while millions have never hear it at all. Sharing Christ and His love with others is the ministry nearest the heart of God. The life-mission of all believers is to tell others how Jesus came and "gave His life a ransom" to redeem them to God.

Chapter 17

Visions To Vanquish Racism

REACHING ALL NATIONS and *every creature* was Christ's mandate to His first followers. But being Jews, it took some supernatural events and visions to convince them that *every creature* and *whosoever* meant "Gentiles," "pagans" or "non-Jews" — as well as Jews.

Their tendency was to restrict their teaching about Christ to Hebraic listeners and not to share it with *unclean, unworthy* Gentiles.

Mandate To All Nations

God created all races equally. Jesus Christ died for the sins of the whole world. *Every creature* has equal value in His sight and therefore deserves to hear His gospel. This is why the church must share Christ with all nations, both genders.

Most of Christ's original followers were Judaeans of Hebraic lineage whose religious traditions forbade association with other races (considered to be *unclean* Gentiles). Therefore, when Jesus ministered to Gentiles the same as He did to Jews, and commissioned His followers to carry His message to *every creature*, it provoked dissent and confusion. Jewish laws forbade them inter-mingling with other races.

God Signals Racial Equality

On the Day of Pentecost, the Holy Spirit came upon all who had been praying in an upper room.[Ac.1:12-14;2:1-4] Overwhelmed by this spiritual phenomenon, Peter arose to explain that it was the fulfillment of what Joel prophesied when he said, *I will pour out my Spirit upon all flesh; and your sons and your daughters shall prophecy...*[Jl.2:28-32]

Speaking under the unction of the Holy Spirit, Peter boldly announced more of Joel's inspired words: **Whosoever** *shall call on the name of the Lord shall be saved.*[Ac.2:21] Obviously, it never occurred to him that this included *Gentiles*. Being a good Judaean, he was thinking that any *Jew* who called on the Lord could be saved.

Peter announced this prophecy to about sixteen different groups or nationalities or races of people identified in the crowd that had gathered.[Ac.2:9-11] The record says that when this outpouring of the Holy Ghost *was noised abroad, the multitude came together, and was confounded, because each one heard those* [believers who had received the Holy Spirit] *speak in their own languages...the wonderful works of God.*[Ac.2:6,11]

What made it puzzling was that *they were all Galilaeans who were speaking...the wonderful works of God.* The crowd knew that those Galilaeans did not speak those languages.[Ac.2:7,11] That fact alone should have indicated to the believers that God wanted His gospel given to *all nations.* But they were so indoctrinated in Judaic tradition that they missed the idea.

Two Special Visions

The tenth chapter of Acts reports more miracles that indicate how much God wanted to heal the racial divisions that restricted His Jewish followers from sharing the good news with *all nations.*

A reputable Gentile named Cornelius had a vision and was told to *send men and call for one Simon, whose surname is Peter,* who would give him further instructions.[Ac.10:1-6]

The next day, as Cornelius' messengers went to Peter's house, he also had a vision[Ac.10:9-10] and was told that three men were coming for him and that he should go with them because the Lord had sent them.[Ac:10:19-20]

The men arrived and told Peter about Cornelius' vision. So he called for some Jewish witnesses to accompany him, and they went with the men to the house of the reputable, but *unclean* Gentile.Ac.10:21-23

When Peter arrived at the door, he explained that rabbinical law forbade him, as a Jew, to enter the house of a Gentile. He said: *You know how it is an unlawful thing for a Jew to keep company, or come unto one of another nation; but God has shown me that I should not call any person common or unclean.*Ac.10:28

This shows how religious rules and scruples can contravene God's will even in the lives of people who want to please Him. It took two visions to get Peter to believe Joel's inspired prophecy that he had announced; **Whosoever** *shall call on the name of the Lord shall be saved.*Ac.2:21 Obviously he never dreamed that this included *Gentiles.*

Peter Enters
Forbidden Terrain

When Peter ventured into the *unclean* Gentile's house, the Lord confirmed his obedience by *sending the Holy Spirit upon all them which heard the word. And they of the circumcision* [Jews] *were astonished, as many as came with Peter* [as witnesses], *because that on the Gentiles also was poured the gift of the Holy Spirit.*Ac.10:45 And they *glorified God, saying, Then has God granted repentance unto life **also to the***

Gentiles.Ac.11:18 This astounded the Jewish believers.

Peter And The Gentiles

Despite these experiences, Peter continued to be cautious about his rapport with Gentiles, apparently trying to cope with religious racism among the Jews. However, when the issue surfaced for official discussion,Ac.15:1-5 *Peter rose up, and* asserted that He was the *first one* to carry the gospel to the Gentiles. He said, *You know how that God made choice among us, that the Gentiles by my mouth should hear the word of the gospel, and believe.*Ac.15:7

Resistance To Gentile Converts

It is amazing how those first apostolic leaders resisted accepting Gentile converts into the family of God, on the same level as Jewish believers. *The apostles that were in Judaea heard that the Gentiles had also received the word of God. And when Peter was come up to Jerusalem, they...contended with him* Ac.11:1-2 because he had gone into the house and had eaten with *uncircumcised* (Gentile) people Ac.11:3

Peter defended himself by recounting his vision and how that *as he began to speak* [at Cornelius' house], *the Holy Ghost had fallen on them, as on* [the one hundred and twenty] *at the beginning.*Ac.11:15

So his defense was: *Forasmuch then as God gave them the like gift as he did unto us, who believed on the Lord Jesus Christ; what was I, that I could withstand God?* Ac.11:17

The Decision At Headquarters

The time had come for those who guided the Early Church to publish a formal decision about this matter that had become such a pivotal issue of contention.

When [James and the other leaders of the church] *heard these things* [Peter's explanation], *they held their peace, and glorified God, saying, Then has God also granted to the **Gentiles** repentance unto life.* Ac.11:18

Despite the formal decision and action taken by James and the elders, racial discrimination stubbornly persisted. While they went on record as approving Gentile converts, none of them took up the torch to run with the gospel message *to the Gentile world.*

God had to raise up a *new convert* and visit him in a miraculous revelation, to convince Jewish believers to carry the gospel to the *non*-Jewish world. The Hebrew followers of Christ were so indoctrinated by Judaic tradition that their interest was limited to *preaching the word to none but the Jews only.* Ac.11:19

Apostle To The Gentiles

One of the most remarkable conversions re-corded in the New Testament is that of *Saul of Tarsus.*[Ac.9:1-22] He had hated the *Christian* cult, approved Stephen's death,[Ac.8:1] and had vengefully witnessed his brutal martyrdom.[Ac.7:58] *He made havock of the church, entering into every house, and haling men and women committed them to prison.*[Ac.8:3]

Saul was a Jew, brought up at the feet of Gamaliel, and taught according to the perfect manner of the law of the fathers, and was zealous toward God, persecuting this way unto the death, binding and delivering into prisons both men and women.[Ac.22:3-4] *He lived after the strictest sect of Jewish religion, a Pharisee.*[Ac.26:5]

Paul testified: *I thought within myself, that I ought to do many things contrary to the name of Jesus of Nazareth...Many of the saints did I shut up in prison, having received authority from the chief priests; and when they were put to death, I gave my voice against them. And I punished them often in every synagogue, and compelled them to blaspheme; and being exceedingly **mad** against them, I persecuted them even unto strange cities.*[Ac.26:9-11]

But after Saul's phenomenal conversion,[Ac.9:] this ex-Pharisee,[Ac.23:6,26:5] led the way in a passionate life-crusade to carry the gospel *to the Gentiles*,[Ac.9:15;13:46;18:6;22:21;28:28; Ga.1:15-16] a cause for which he suffered persecution, hardship, privation, shame and brutal torture,[2Co.4:8-10;11:23-27; Ac.13:50;14:19;]

255

16:22-24;22:22-25; 2Ti.3:10-12 and for which he laid down his life,Ep.3:1; 2Ti.4:6-7 being executed at Rome in late A.D. 66 or early 67.

Revelation of Redemption

*Saul, who is also called Paul*Ac.13:9 was the man who received the revelation of salvation through grace and faith in Jesus Christ,Ga.1:11-12;2:16;4:4-5;6:14; Ac.15:11; Ep.2:8-9; Ro.3:24 without the works of the Mosaic law.Ga.2:16;3:11; Ro.3:20-22 He led the way in proving that there could be no racial or sexual discrimination in God's plan of redemption. He said, *There is neither **Jew nor Greek** [Gentile], there is neither **bond nor free**, there is neither **male nor female**: for you are all one in Christ Jesus.*Ga.3:28

Paul is the one who combined Hebraic believers with Gentile converts wherever he witnessed of Christ, establishing that the message of God's love and redemption was truly for *all nations, and kindreds, and people, and tongues,*Re.7:9 and that *the everlasting gospel is to be preached unto them that dwell on the earth, to every nation, and kindred, and tongue and people.*Re.14:6

Judaean Resistance

Jesus had said *that repentance and remission of sins should be preached in his name among **all** nations,*Lu.24:47; Mt.28:19 *to **all** the world, to **every** creature,*Mk.16:15 and *unto the **uttermost** part of the earth.*Ac.1:8

Yet, despite His explicit commands, Hebraic believers of Judea still repulsed Paul's teaching that Gentiles and Jews were the same in God's sight.

Paul did his best to influence the *churches of God in Judaea*[1Th.2:14] who had suffered great persecution from *the Jews*[1Th.2:14-15] – both by those who rejected Christ as their Messiah, and by those who embraced Him but did not believe that Gentiles were equal in God's sight with the Jews. Paul said that those Judeans *forbid us to speak to the Gentiles that they might be saved.*[1Th.2:16]

Some of the Jews were so aggressive in their opposition to Paul's ministry to Gentiles, that he *prayed to God that he might be delivered from them in Judaea that do not believe.*[Ro.15:30-31]

Jews Demand That Gentiles Obey The Laws Of Moses

It seems that the majority of Jews who embraced Jesus as Messiah insisted that Gentile converts conform to rabbinical law. If they were to be part of the Christian community, then Judaic believers demanded that they obey the law of Moses.

Paul and Barnabas reported to the new Christian community in Antioch about *how God had opened the door of faith to the Gentiles.* And as soon as this news reached the Judaean believers, *certain men came down from Judaea and taught that, Except*

257

you be circumcised after the manner of Moses, **you cannot be saved.**Ac.15:1 *And they had no small dissension and disputation with them.*Ac.15:2 They never slackened their opposition until dear brothers Paul and Barnabas had to make a journey all the way to Jerusalem to defend their ministry and *declare the conversion of the Gentiles.*Ac.15:3

The Great Dispute

But there rose up certain of the sect of the Pharisees **which believed**, *saying, That it was needful to circumcise* [those Gentile converts], *and to command them to keep the law of Moses.*Ac.15:5 *And there was much disputing.*Ac.15:7

Paul and Barnabas argued that *God, which knows the hearts, gave them the Holy Ghost, even as He did unto us; and put* **no difference** *between us and them, purifying their hearts by faith.*Ac.15:8-9 To further validate their argument, they *declared what miracles and wonders God had wrought among the Gentiles* Ac.15:12 and insisted that *through the grace of the Lord Jesus Christ, they would be saved, even as* [the Jews who believed.] Ac.15:11

Paul Rebukes Peter

Paul and Peter differed about this issue. Peter seemed to be secretive in his rapport with Gentile converts, while Paul was open about the matter. He rebuked Peter publicly, saying: *When Peter came to Antioch, I withstood him to the face, because he was to be blamed.*^{Ga.2:11}

Paul explained how Peter and some Jewish believers had visited in the homes of Gentiles and had even eaten with them. But, when representatives from the headquarters church at Jerusalem came to investigate Paul about ministering to the Gentiles, Peter and his Jewish friends broke off their contacts with the Gentiles, evidently to avoid being reported to the Jerusalem church.

Paul strongly opposed their secrecy. He explained: *For before certain men came from James [head of the Jerusalem church], Peter would eat with the Gentiles;* ^{Ga.2:12NKJV} *but when they came, he withdrew and separated himself, fearing those who were of the circumcision [Jewish believers]. And the rest of the Jews also played the hypocrite with him, so that even Barnabas was carried away with their hypocrisy.*^{Ga.2:12-13NKJV}

Then Paul continues: *When I saw that [Peter and his Jewish friends] were not straightforward about the truth of the gospel, I said to Peter before them all, If you, being a Jew, live in the manner of Gentiles and not as Jews, why do you compel Gentiles to live as Jews?* ^{Ga.2:14NKJV} We know that *no one is justified by the works of the law, but by the faith of Jesus Christ.* ^{Ga.2:16} *If righteousness comes by the law, then **Christ is dead in vain**.*^{Ga.2:21}

Paul Contends:
"There Is No Difference!"

Such strong contention between apostles like Peter and Paul reveals how inflexible racial bigotry was among Judaic believers. It illustrates why supernatural intervention was all that persuaded them to eventually *accept* Gentile converts.

In spite of the many *wonders* that signaled the importance of taking the gospel to the Gentile world, none of the believing Jews were ready to identify themselves in Gentile evangelism.

To motivate giving the gospel to *all races*, God miraculously revealed Christ to a self-righteous Pharisee named Saul, a fanatical persecutor of Christians, and spoke to him in an audible voice, *specifically calling him to take the gospel to the Gentiles.*[Ac.9:3-19]

No wonder Paul made such strong statements: *There is **no difference** between the Jew and the Greek [Gentile]: for the same Lord over **all** is rich unto **all** that call upon him. For **whosoever** shall call upon the name of the Lord shall be saved.*[Ro.10:12-13]

Paul insisted that anyone who embraces Jesus as Lord would be *renewed in knowledge after the image of him that created him or her: where there is neither Greek [Gentile] nor Jew, circumcision nor uncircumcision, Barbarian, Scythian, bond nor free:* **but Christ is all, and in all.**Col.3:10-11

Peter To The Jews
Paul To The Gentiles

Peter's vision caused him to be the *first* to give God's word to the Gentiles.Ac.10:9-10;15:7 That experience left him convinced that Gentiles were equal with Jews in God's sight. But to avoid clashing with the Jerusalem church where Jewish influence was strong, he tried to conceal from the Jerusalem *brethren* his rapport with Gentile converts, and Paul felt that his action was a betrayal. So, apparently he never depended again on Peter's alliance regarding Gentile ministry. He simply agreed with Peter's choice to minister to the Jews.

There is an interesting fact to be observed here. After the conference where Paul rebuked Peter for being secretive about his rapport with Gentile converts, but where Peter defended himself as being the *first* messenger to the Gentiles,Ac.15: nothing more is said in the Acts of the Apostles about Peter. With the opening of the door to the Gentiles, Peter receded into the background and *Paul became prominent as the apostle to the Gentiles.*

Paul was gracious about the matter. He knew that the leaders at Jerusalem were in agreement that *the gospel for the* **un***circumcised* [Gentiles] *had* *been committed to Paul.* Of course Paul had been determined to reach the Gentile world with the gospel. He knew it was vastly larger than the limited world of religious Jews. The Jerusalem leaders agreed that *the gospel for the circumcised* [Jews] *was committed to Peter.*

Paul graciously acquiesced to this thinking. He wrote, *God who works effectively in Peter for the apostleship to the Jews also works effectively in me toward the Gentiles.*[Ga.2:7-8NKJV] So He was content to leave the matter at that, convinced that *his* was the broader ministry that extended the gospel to a broader world, a ministry *un*restrained by racial or sexual or national limitations. Paul was a *redemption* thinker. In his mind, Christ died for *everyone,* and *whosoever* would believe on Him would be saved without any adherence to the Old Testament law of Moses that Jewish believers were still preoccupied with.

James, the head of the church,[Ac.12:17;15:13;21:18; Ga.2:12] with the elders, heard the dispute between Peter and Paul, and also arguments by the Jewish disciples who contended that *Gentiles must be circumcised and follow the law of Moses.*

To resolve the matter, James rehearsed the details of Peter's vision and of his visiting Cornelius' house.[Ac.15:13-14] Then he assured them that he believed that Peter's action *agreed with the words of the prophets.*[Ac.15:15]

Decision From Headquarters

So James formally issued *his sentence* [Ac.15:19] that [Jewish Christians no longer] *trouble the Gentiles who are turning to God.*[Ac.15:19]

He then instructed that letters be provided, to be carried by Paul and Barnabas and read to all Gentile believers and new converts, giving them official assurance that they would be accepted as fellow-believers in Christian communities and as worthy followers of Jesus Christ.

They wrote: *The apostles and elders and brethren send greetings to...the Gentiles...because we have heard that some went out from us and troubled you with words, subverting your souls, saying, You must be circumcised, and keep the law.*[Ac.15:23-24]

Then the letter assured the Gentiles that *we gave no such command*[Ac.15:24] and announced that the elders officially approve the ministry of *our beloved Barnabas and Paul, as men who have hazarded their lives* [taking the gospel to the Gentiles] *for the name of our Lord Jesus Christ.*[Ac.15:.25-26]

The Living Bible makes it very clear. Paul says: *When the pillars of the church saw how greatly God had used me in winning the Gentiles, just as Peter had been blessed so greatly in his preaching to the Jews — for the same God gave us each our special gifts — they shook hands with Barnabas and me and encouraged us* to keep right on with our preaching to the Gentiles while they continued their work with the Jews.[Ga.2:7-9LB]

Paul Contends:
Gentiles And Jews Are The Same

Because of Paul's miraculous conversion[Ac.9:3-20] and his audible call from the Lord to *bear his name before the Gentiles,*[Ac.9:15;26:17] he never questioned the race issue again, but paid a great price and suffered humiliation, opposition and persecution to faithfully fulfill the ministry he believed God had chosen him for.[Ga.1:15-16]

He made unmitigated and unequivocal statements about his ministry: *I am the apostle of the Gentiles, and I magnify my office.*[Ro.11:13] *I am a minister of Jesus Christ to the Gentiles, ministering the gospel of God.*[Ro.15:16] *I am ordained...a teacher of the Gentiles in faith and verity.*[1Ti.2:7] *I am appointed...a teacher of the Gentiles.*[2Ti.1:11]

Paul was persistent in contending that **the gospel of Christ is for all races and for both genders.**

We testify both to the Jews, and to the Greeks [Gentiles], repentance toward God, and faith toward our Lord Jesus Christ.[Ac.20:21] *Be it known unto you, that the salvation of God is sent unto the Gentiles.*[Ac.28:28] *Is he the God of the Jews only? Is he not also of the Gentiles? Yes, of the Gentiles also.*[Ro.3:29]

God made known the riches of his glory...even to us, whom he has called, not of the Jews only, but also of the Gentiles.Ro.9:23-24

Christ redeemed us...so that the blessing of Abraham might come on the Gentiles through Jesus Christ.Ga.3:13-14

By revelation God made known to me...that the Gentiles should be fellowheirs, and of the same body, and partakers of his promise in Christ by the gospel. Ep.3:3,6

Cruelty Of Racism

Racism, like sexism is a cruel and bigoted mental perspective that views one race or tribe or color or gender as superior to another. That bias infected the early church and, unfortunately, still affects the attitudes and conduct of people today—a behavioral disposition foreign to biblical Christianity.

Paul's contention was that by one Spirit are we all baptized into one body, whether we be Jews or Gentiles, whether we be bond or free; and have been all made to drink into one Spirit.1Co.12:13 There is neither Jew nor Greek [Gentile], there is neither bond nor free, there is neither male nor female: for you are all one in Christ Jesus.Ga.3:29

Paul was a pioneer in teaching the redemptive equality of races and of sexes. Under his apostolate, both men and women believers carried the message of Christ throughout their world, to both Jews and Gentiles of both genders, which was God's plan when He *so loved the world, that he gave his only begotten Son, that **whoever** believes in him should not perish, but have everlasting life.*Jn.3:16

✧ ✧ ✧

IN THE FOLLOWING chapters we shall look at vital truths which First Century believers cherished — that made them world-changers. Then we shall see how those truths were lost during the Dark Ages.

But in each case, we shall see that believers today are in the process of, or have already rediscovered those dynamic truths, and that they are producing the greatest soul harvests in the history of the Church.

Chapter 18

Faith For Salvation

PERSONAL FAITH FOR salvation was the heartbeat of every First Century Christian's relationship with God. By the Third Century, this vibrant faith was superseded by ecclesiastical imperialism that continued to dominate throughout the Dark Ages. The concept of *individual faith in God* was not rebirthed in the lives of people until after Martin Luther's Reformation was seeded by his 95 Theses in 1517.

First Century Christains believed that *the gospel is the power of God unto salvation **to everyone that believes**; to the Jew first, and also to the Greek* [Gentile].^{Ro.1:16} They believed that *by grace are you saved **through faith**; and that not of yourselves: it is the gift of God: Not of works, lest anyone should boast;* ^{Ep.2:8-9} that *the just shall live **by faith**.*^{Hab.2:4; Ro.1:17;} ^{Ga.3:11; He.10:38}

That simple faith in Christ was finally extinguished under the ecclesiastical subjugation of people by the political-religious hierarchy. Martin

Luther's Reformation in 1517 was principally a revolt against State-Church domination and a challenge for believers to examine the scriptures for themselves—something that had been forbidden by church pontificates for centuries.

As people rediscovered the scriptures for themselves by reading them, faith for salvation was created in their hearts and they began to experience the reality of Jesus Christ in their lives. Being a Christian was no longer a formal affiliation with the ecclesiastical order called *The Church*, but it was once again a living, vital relationship with Jesus Christ.

52 Facts Of Salvation

CREATE A VISUAL OF THE 52.

IN THE LAST CHAPTER of this book, we will present the significance of this living faith for salvation. It was treasured by First Century believers, but then it was lost during the Dark Ages. Now it has been rediscovered since the Reformation. In this 18th chapter, we are setting forth 52 facts about this faith that are fundamental to knowing Christ and to walking with Him.

1. We were *unsaved* before we received Christ. *For all have sinned, and come short of the glory of God.*[Ro.3:23]

2. We were guilty before God, under the penalty of death. *For the wages of sin is death.*[Ro.6:23]

3. But God loved us too much to see us perish. *He is not willing that any should perish but that all should come to repentance.*2Pe.3:9

4. God offered His best to prove His love for us. *He so loved the world that he gave his only begotten Son, that whoever believes in him should not perish, but have everlasting life.*Jn.3:16

5. Christ was God's gift to us and He died for you and for me. *But God commends his love toward us, in that, while we were yet sinners, Christ died for us.*Ro.5:8

6. We realize that our sins had separated us from God. *Your iniquities have separated between you and your God, and your sins have hid his face from you.*Is.59:2

7. Knowing that our sins cost God His Son, and Jesus His life and blood, we repent of them. *You sorrowed to repentance...for godly sorrow works repentance,*2Co.7:9-10 and you know that *except you repent you shall perish.*Lu.13:3

8. We confess our sins to Him and are cleansed. *If we confess our sins, he is faithful and just to forgive us our sins, and to cleanse us from all unrighteousness.*1Jn.1:9

9. We recognize Jesus at the door of our heart. We open it and He comes in. *Behold, I stand at the door, and knock: if you hear my voice, and open the*

door, I will come in and will sup with you and you with me [dine together and have fellowship].Rev.3:20

10. We receive Jesus and become God's child. *As many as received Jesus Christ, to them he gave power to become the children of God, even to them that believe on his name.*Jn.1:12

11. We become a new creature. *If any one be in Christ, that one is a new creature: old things are passed away; behold, all things are become new.*2Co.5:17

12. We know we are born again because we receive Christ. Jesus said, *You must be born again,*Jn.3:7 *and when you received Christ with power to become God's child,*Jn.1:12 *you were born, not of blood, nor of the will of the flesh, nor of the will of a human being, but of God,*Jn.1:13 *by the word of God, which lives and abides for ever.*1Pe.1:23

13. We believe the powerful message of the gospel that saves us. *The gospel...is the power of God to salvation to every one that believes.*Ro.1:16

14. We believe on the name of Jesus Christ because of the record of the gospels. *These are written, that you might believe that Jesus is the Christ, the Son of God; and that believing, you might have life through his name.*Jn.20:31

15. We call on His name and we are saved. *Whoever shall call on the name of the Lord shall be saved.*Ro.10:13

16. We recognize that Jesus is the only way to God. *I am the way, the truth, and the life; no one comes to the Father, but by me,*Jn.14:6 *for there is one God, and one mediator between God and people, the man Christ Jesus.*1Ti.2:5

17. We know there is salvation in none other. *Neither is there salvation in any other: for there is none other name under heaven given, whereby we must be saved.*Ac.4:12

18. We put our faith in Jesus as our personal savior. *For by grace are you saved through faith; and that not of yourselves; it is the gift of God: not of works, lest any one should boast.*Ep.2:8-9

19. We believe that the Lord comes into our life. *I will dwell in them, and walk in them; and I will be their God, and they shall be my people...I will be a Father to you, and you shall be my sons and daughters, says the Lord Almighty.*2Co.6:16,18

20. We do not trust in any good works of self-righteousness to be saved. *Our righteousnesses are as filthy rags,*Is.64:6 Your salvation was *not of works, lest any one should boast.*Ep.2:9

21. We are saved only by God's mercy. *Not by works of righteousness which we have done, but according to his mercy he saved us, by the washing of regeneration, and renewing of the Holy Spirit; which he shed on us abundantly through Jesus Christ our savior; that being justified by grace, we should be made heirs according to the hope of eternal life.*Tit.3:5-7

22. We know Christ's death justifies us before God. *Being justified by faith, we have peace with God through our Lord Jesus Christ.*[Ro.5:1]

23. We know His blood remits (removes, eradicates and absolves from punishment) our sins forever. *This is my blood...which is shed for many for the remission of sins.*[Mt.26:28]

24. We know we are cleansed from sin. *To him that loved us, and washed us from our sins in his own blood;*[Re.1:5] *in whom we have redemption through his blood, even the forgiveness of sins.*[Col.1:14]

25. We know our sins are put away and forgotten. *Behold the Lamb of God, which takes away the sins of the world,*[Jn.1:29] *having removed our transgressions from us as far as the east is from the west,*[Ps.103:12] *so that our sins and iniquities will he remember no more.*[He.10:17]

26. We know our sins were paid for by Christ's death. *Who his own self bore our sins in his own body on the tree, that we, being dead to sins, should live unto righteousness.*[1Pe.2:24] *He was wounded for our transgressions. He was bruised for our iniquities: the chastisement of our peace was upon him.*[Is.53:5]

27. With our sins punished and expunged, we know they can never condemn us again. *There is therefore now no condemnation to them which are in Christ Jesus,*[Ro.8:1] *for God made him who knew no sin, to be sin for us; that we might be made the righteousness of God in Christ,*[2Co.5:21] *and where remission is,*

there is no more offering for sin,[He.10:18] so that now nothing *shall separate us from the love of Christ.*[Ro.8:35-39]

28. We know when we accept Christ that we receive His life. *Those who have the Son have life,*[1Jn.5:12] for *they that hear my word, and believe on him that sent me, have everlasting life, and shall not come into condemnation but are passed from death to life.*[Jn.5:24] *And this is life eternal, that they might know you the only true God, and Jesus Christ whom you have sent.*[Jn.17:3]

29. We know Satan will accuse us. *He is the accuser which accused them before our God day and night* [Re.12:10] just like he did Job.[Job1:6-12]

30. We are not ignorant of Satan's works. *Lest Satan should get an advantage of us: for we are not ignorant of his devices.*[2Co.2:11] For we know that he comes not, but to steal, and to kill, and to destroy.*[Jn.10:10]

31. We know how Jesus overcame him. *But he answered and said, it is written...*[Mt.4:4,7,10] *Then the devil left him, and, behold, angels came and ministered to him.*[Mt.4:11]

32. We know Jesus proved that Satan could not win. *Christ was in all points tempted like we are, yet without sin. Let us therefore come boldly to the throne of grace, that we may obtain mercy, and find grace to help in time of need.*[He.4:15-16]

33. We know He faithfully helps us in temptation. *There is no temptation taken you but such as is
common to humankind: but God is faithful, who will
not suffer you to be tempted above that you are able;
but will with the temptation also make a way to escape,
that you may be able to bear it.*[1Co.10:13]

34. We know that there are two weapons Satan
can never resist. *And they overcame him* [the devil
who accused them before God day and night] *by
the blood of the Lamb, and by the word of their testimony.*[Re.12:11]

35. We know Satan cannot win over our faith.
*Be sober, be vigilant; because your adversary the devil,
as a roaring lion, walks about, seeking whom he may
devour: whom resist steadfast in the faith.*[1Pe.5:8-9] *Resist
the devil, and he will flee from you. Draw nigh to God,
and he will draw nigh to you;*[Ja.4:7-8] *but the begotten of
God keep themselves, and that wicked one touches
them not.*[1Jn.5:18]

36. We know our faith is the victory. *For whoever
is born of God overcomes the world: and this is the victory that overcomes the world, even our faith.*[1Jn.5:4]

37. We know not to love the world but to do
God's will. *Love not the world, neither the things that
are in the world. If any one loves the world, the love of
the Father is not in them. For all that is in the world,
the lust of the flesh, and the lust of the eyes, and the
pride of life, is not of the Father, but is of the world.*

And the world passes away, and the lust thereof: but those that do the will of God abide for ever.[1Jn.2:15-17]

38. We know Christ came to defeat our enemy. *For this purpose the Son of God was manifested, that he might destroy the works of the devil.*[1Jn.3:8]

39. We know Satan is no match for Christ in us. *Christ in you, the hope of glory.*[Col.1:27] *I will dwell in you and walk in you...says the Lord Almighty.*[2Co.6:16,18] *You are of God, little children, and have overcome...because greater is he that is in you, than he that is in the world.*[1Jn.4:4]

40. We know our new life source is the Lord Jesus Christ. *I am crucified with Christ: nevertheless I live; yet not I, but Christ lives in me: and the life which I now live in the flesh I live by the faith of the Son of God, who loved me, and gave himself for me.*[Ga.2:20]

41. We know our new life has divine purpose. *The steps of good people are ordered by the Lord: and God delights in their ways. Though they fall, they shall not be utterly cast down: for the Lord upholds them with his hand.*[Ps.37:23-24]

42. We know God sees us and hears us. *For the eyes of the Lord are over the righteous, and his ears are open to their prayers.*[1Pe.3:12]

43. We know that He invites us to call upon Him. *Call unto me, and I will answer you.*[Je.33:3] *Ask, and it shall be given you; seek, and you shall find;*

knock, and it shall·be opened to you. For everyone that asks receives.[Lu.11:9-10]

44. We know when we pray that He answers. *Whatever you desire, when you pray, believe that you receive them, and you shall have them;*[Mk.11:24] *and whatever you shall ask in my name, that will I do, that the Father may be glorified in the Son.*[Jn.14:13]

45. We know that we belong to God's royal family. *You are a chosen generation, a royal priesthood, an holy nation, a peculiar people; that you should show forth the praises of him who has called you out of darkness into his marvelous light.*[1Pe.2:9]

46. We know that all that Christ has now belongs to us. *For all who are led by the Spirit of God are children of God. And so we should not be like cringing, fearful slaves, but we should behave like God's very own children, adopted into the bosom of his family, and calling to him, 'Father, Father,' for his Holy Spirit speaks to us deep in our hearts, and tells us that we really are God's children. And since we are his children, we will share his treasures — for all God gives to his Son Jesus is now ours too.*[Ro.8:14-17LB]

47. We know we have His life in our flesh now. *That the life of Jesus might be made manifest in our mortal flesh,*[2Co.4:11] *for your body is the temple of the Holy Spirit.*[1Co.3:16-17]

48. We know we never need to live in want again. *My God shall supply all your need according to his riches in glory by Christ Jesus,*[Ph.4:19] *for no good*

*thing will he withhold from them that walk up-rightly.*Ps.84:11

49. We no longer fear diseases and plagues. *There shall no evil befall you, neither shall any plague come nigh your dwelling,*Ps.91:10 *because I am the Lord that heals you.*Ex.15:26 *Jesus took our infirmities and bore our sicknesses,*Mt.8:17 *and with his stripes we are healed.*Is.53:5; 1Pe.2:24

50. We no longer are oppressed by problems. *Casting all your care upon him; for he cares for you.*1Pe.5:7

51. We know that we are winners. *For if God be for us, who can be against us?* Ro.8:31 *Nay, in all these things we are more than conquerors through him that loved us.*Ro.8:37 *He which has begun a good work in you will perform it until the day of Jesus Christ;*Ph.1:6 *and Faithful is he that calls you, who also will do it.*1Th.5:24

52. We know Christ is with us to the end. *For he has said, I will never leave you, nor forsake you. So that we may boldly say, The Lord is my helper, and I will not fear what any person shall do to me,*He.13:5-6 *and, lo, I am with you alway, even to the end of the world.*Mt.28:20

◇ ◇ ◇

THESE ARE THE FACTS of the gospel that we are to share with our world. These 52 truths can be a great help in sharing the Jesus-life with others.

The following prayer can be a guide to help anyone to accept Jesus Christ into their life as personal savior and Lord. If you have not yet embraced Him as a living reality in your own life, then — PRAY THIS PRAYER:

Prayer Of Faith

OH HEAVENLY FATHER, I am thankful to know and understand the gospel and to believe what it says. I believe on Jesus Christ and, by faith, I receive you, dear Lord, as my personal savior — *now*.

You were without sin,[He.9:28; 1Pe.2:22] yet you died for my sins.[1Co.15:2; 1Pe.2:24] You took my place, assumed my judgment and suffered my penalty in order to ransom me and to restore me to God as though I had never sinned.[Is.53:4-5; Re1:5; 5:9; Ro.5:1]

You took my sins and now, by accepting you, you impart to me your righteousness.[2Co.5:21] I have come to realize what a great price you paid to prove how much you value me. Your blood was shed to ransom me.[Ro.5:8-9]

OH JESUS, MY LORD, since you paid the full price for my transgressions, there can never be any further price to pay, nor any further penalty or judgment to suffer.[He.10:8] I believe that I am saved, now and forever, because of the good news of what you accomplished for me when you died in my place.

Now I am restored to God my Father through Jesus my savior. I have recovered the dignity you planned for me. I do believe that you have now come to live in me like you originally planned when you created me.

I believe I am saved.[Ep.2:8] You and I are *one* again because of what your Son, Jesus, did in my place. The blood of Jesus Christ cleanses me.[1Jn.1:7] The life of Jesus Christ regenerates me.[1Pe.1:23] The joy of Jesus Christ fills me.[Jn.15:11]

I am of infinite value.[1Pe.1:7] Thank you that you love me. I am yours.[Jn.6:37] You have made my body your temple.[1Co.6:19-20] I am redeemed and accepted. I have become a representative of the Kingdom of God in this life.[2Co.5:19-21]

MY SINS ARE PUNISHED. They can never be punished again.[He.9:11-12,28;10:12-14,17-22] My debt is paid. No debt can ever be paid twice. I am saved—here and now.[2Co.6:2] I believe that, and I am free.[Jn.8:32,36; 2Co.3:17; Ro.8:32]

Thank you, Lord, for the power that makes me your child,[Jn.1:12] and that makes me a new creature [2Co.5:17] now that I have welcomed you to live in me. Now I am as valuable to you as anyone else in the world because you paid the same price for me that you paid for any other person. I am as beautiful in your eyes as anyone can be. I am loved. I can love others. Whatever I sow in others, I will reap in multiplied form.[Ga.6:7]

Thank you that I am part of your plan now. I have a place that no one else can fill.[Ep.2:10] No longer will I condemn myself.[Ro.8:1; Jn.3:17; 5:24] No longer will I demean or destroy what you esteem so highly.[1Co.6:20]

Now I am accepted in your family[Ep.1:6] I can do your work.[Jn.14:12;20:21; 1Co.3:9; 2Co.3:5-6] I am born again.[Jn.3:3; 1Pe.1:23] I am a new creature.[2Co.5:17] I have repented of my old values. I have changed my mind about myself and about other people. Knowing how you value each human person has given me a new value of human life.[Ga.1:4; Tit.2:14; Re.1:5;5:9]

I SEE YOU, Oh Lord, with new eyes.[Ps.34:2-7;21:6; 119:135; Ac.2:25-26,28; He.12:2-3] I see others now as you see them. I see myself in your own image.[Ge.1:26-27; Ps.8:4-6] Together with you, I can never fail.[He.13:5; Ph.4:13; Lu.1:37; Mk.9:23; Ps.27:1] Thank you Lord, that you live in me.[Col.1:27; Ga.2:20; 2Co.6:16; Jn.14:20; 15:7] In Jesus' name. AMEN!

❖ ❖ ❖

THIS IS THE *faith that was once delivered to the saints.*[Jude1:3] This is *the victory that overcomes the world, even our faith.*[1Jn.5:4] Martin Luther's Reformation caused Christians to read the scriptures for themselves, which are the source of *faith* [that] comes by hearing the word of God.[Ro.10:17]

Next, we shall look at First Century mass evangelism, at why it disappeared during the Dark Ages, then at its reappearance in the 1700s.

Chapter 19

Mass Evangelism

MASS EVANGELISM, witnessing of Christ to great crowds out in public places, is another aspect of First Century ministry that was extinguished during the Dark Ages, and did not reappear until during the 1700s, under John Wesley's evangelism ministry. Jesus had preached to the multitudes and His followers had emulated His example whenever there was freedom to do so, but then it was suppressed and finally stifled by the imposing bureaucracy of State religion.

Peter witnessed to multitudes in Jerusalem,[Ac.3:11; 4:4;5:12-16] Lydda, and Saron,[Ac.9:32-35] Philip in Samaria,[Ac.8:4-8] Paul in Antioch,[Ac.13:44] Iconium,[14:1] Jerusalem,[15:12] Thessalonica,[17:4] Athens,[17:16,22] and in many other chief cities.

But this kind of ministry disappeared after Christianity became popular in the Roman Empire. When Emperor Constantine proclaimed his conversion, then he assumed the role of spiritual head of the Christian Church. As a result, the spirit of evangelism was extinguished.

Pontifical edicts restricted Christian teaching to *sacred* sanctuaries and forbade its instruction in *secular* venues. Public evangelism could not exist under Roman ecclesiastical rule, and it did not return until the ministry of the great British preacher, John Wesley.

Wesley had been disqualified from formal church institutions because of his public proclamation of the gospel. He took the good news of Christ out into places that the institutional Church considered *profane* and *impious*, such as fields, cemeteries, parks and roadways, out where thousands of common people could hear the gospel and learn of Christ. Although this was fundamental in Early Church ministry, Wesley was vehemently opposed by pontificating Church clerics of his day.

Heretics In Profane Places

The Church Hierarchy of Wesley's epoch considered that his preaching out in public, secular environments, was a desecration of the gospel, that it was *heretical,* and a serious *vulgarization of Sacred Writ.* Tradition dictated that the sanctity of God's word forbade it being taught to *un*regenerate *commoners* out in public places. That was considered to be like *throwing bread to common dogs in the street.*

Through the sacrifice and persistence of Wesley and others, public evangelism was finally approved by the Church and it became the catalyst for spreading the gospel across new world frontiers by pioneers like Wesley, Whitfield, Finney, Spurgeon, Moody and many others.

In chapter 16, we shared an overview of our own experiences in scores of nations as we followed the early church's example of mass, public evangelism confirmed by signs and miracles. [Ac.4:33;6:7;8:4-8,12;12:21,24;13:48-49;14:3;15:12;26:18;Ro.15:18-19;He.2:4]

While the above-named evangelism pioneers proclaimed the gospel to great public crowds, they never seemed to think of reaching the *une*vangelized millions of *non*-Christian nations. Nor did they re-introduce healing miracles to convince the *un*converted of the reality of Jesus and the truth of the Bible.

Miracle Evangelism Pioneers

Daisy and I were the first gospel messengers, since those of the Early Church, *to publicly proclaim Christ in non-Christian nations, out in parks, stadiums, and terrains where people of all religions could hear the gospel and see it confirmed by healing miracles, like those recorded in the Bible.*

Wesley pioneered proclaiming the gospel out in public places in the **Christian world**. *We* pioneered public evangelism in the *non*-**Christian world**. We invited the public to come, to hear and see for themselves that Christ is alive and that the Bible is true. *Jesus was approved of God* [in Bible days] *by miracles and wonders and signs, which God did by him.*[Ac.2:22] We believed that God would give the same proof of Christ today, and that multitudes would believe on Him if we *preached...the Lord working with us, confirming the word with signs following.*[Mk.16:20]

We have now proven in over eighty nations that once people are offered an opportunity to hear the gospel *in demonstration of the Spirit and of power,*[1Co.2:4] they will believe it and eagerly respond to embrace faith in Jesus Christ.

✧ ✧ ✧

IN OUR NEXT chapter, we shall look at how the *missionary* vision of Christ's followers *to reach all nations with the gospel* flourished in First Century Christianity, but how it became extinct during the Dark Ages, then how, after fourteen long centuries, it was rediscovered and how it flourishes again in this century.

Chapter 20

Missions—To All Races

THE MISSIONARY VISION of First Century Christians was lost during the Dark Ages and was not rediscovered for at least fourteen long centuries. Early believers lived with a passion to *preach the gospel to every creature, in all the world,* in preparation for Jesus Christ to return.

Luke's record of the Acts of the Apostles has preserved valuable accounts of the ministries of Peter, Philip, Stephen, Barnabas, Silas, Mark, and mainly of the leading apostle to the Gentiles, Paul.[Ro.11:13; 1Ti.2:7; 2Ti.1:11]

Extra-biblical Reports

Other documentations of the exploits of faith and of the journeys of early apostles and of other believers exist in various historical records such as the fourth century *Ecclesiastical History* by Bishop Eusebius of Caesarea. He records missions by *Bartholomew* into Parthia (in modern

Iran), Ethiopia, Mesopotamia, Lycaonia (in modern Turkey), and Armenia.

The bishop's *History* gives accounts of *Tomas* evangelizing in Parthia (also known as Khorasan —an area of southern Russia, northern Afghanistan and northeastern Iran), and how he journeyed all the way into south India where he is recognized as the founder of the Church of the Syrian Malabar Christians.

Andrew, according to early church legends, pushed northward in his missionary activities around the Black Sea, nations now known as Bulgaria, Romania, Maldavia, the Ukraine, southern Russia, and Georgia, with Turkey spanning the southern shoreline.

Early stories about *Philip* tell of his evangelizing ministry in the ancient Eurasian area of Scythia, north of the Black Sea and east of the Ural Sea, a people renowned for their prowess in war who had migrated northward from Iran.

Scanty information and legends about *Matthew* give glimpses of his missions into Ethiopia and eastward across Persia (Iran).

Simon the Zealot is reported to have carried out evangelism missions into Egypt, after which he is said to have joined with *Thaddaeus* in spreading the gospel across Persia (Iran).

These are only a few remnants of legendary accounts which have been preserved about some of the twelve apostles. Though fragmentary, they indicate thousands of unrecorded stories of heroic efforts made by early Christians to propagate the gospel in all directions.

Paul's Special Call

The apostle Paul invested his life going to the Gentile nations of the Roman Empire, proclaiming the gospel and establishing his new converts, both Jews and Greeks (or Gentiles), into believing communities.[Ac.14:1;18:4;19:10,17;20:21; 1Co.1:24]

At Paul's conversion, God spoke to Ananias about him saying, *he is a chosen vessel unto me, to bear my name before the Gentiles.*[Ac.9:15] And the Lord said to Paul himself, *I have appeared to you for this purpose, to make you a minister and a witness...I am sending you to the Gentiles, to open their eyes, and to turn them from darkness to light, from the power of Satan unto God, that they might receive the forgiveness of sins...*[Ac.26:16-18]

That is why Paul wrote: *I am a debtor to the Greeks, and to the Barbarians; both to the wise, and to the unwise.*[Ro.1:14] He kept insisting that salvation was for both Jews and Gentiles,[Ro.1:16;10:12; Ga.3:28; Col.3:11] emphasizing that *the salvation of God is sent to the Gentiles.*[Ac.28:28]

So while this apostle to the *Gentiles* proclaimed Christ across the Roman Empire, his example of sharing Christ with the Gentiles evidently had a strong influence on other believers and Christian leaders who penetrated other nations of their world with the gospel. Thousands of exploits for Christ will never be known because those gallant messengers laid down their lives reaching these remote and uncivilized areas of the world.

Jewish Opposition

Almost everywhere Paul went in his heroic missionary journeys, he was trailed by Jews who resented the fact that he, a learned Jewish Pharisee, trained by Gamaliel,[Ac.22:3;26:4-5] was out preaching the Abrahamic covenant, the Mosaic law, the Psalms and the Prophets to *Gentile* peoples, desecrating sacred scriptures by using them to identify Jesus as the savior of such *unclean* people.

Other Jews who had embraced Christ as their Messiah, but who still clung to rabbinical discrimination against other races, also opposed Paul. Whenever they heard that he had won Gentiles to Christ, even in distant cities, they rushed messengers to harass him, and often provoked terrible persecution.[Ac.13:44-50;14:1-2,5,19;17:4-5,13,17; 18:12-13;21:11-12,19-21,27-28;22:19-22;24:5;25:2,7,24;26:2,21; 2Co.11:23-27]

Christ's commission to teach God's redemptive blessings to all peoples of all races and of both sexes, was to the Jews the same as *casting pearls before swine*. The idea was antagonistic to *sacred* rabbinical teaching.

But Paul was setting a new standard for the followers of Jesus. Many of them could remember how their Lord had shown compassion to people of all races and of both sexes.

"Inclusiveness"
The Hallmark Of Christianity

This apostle to the Gentiles firmly established human *inclusiveness* as the hallmark of New Testament Christianity. Paul insisted that *we are all the children of God by faith in Christ Jesus...There is neither **Jew nor Greek**, there is neither **bond nor free**, there is neither **male nor female**: for we are all one in Christ Jesus.*[Ga.3:26,28]

That passion to announce God's salvation to all people of all nations caused those First Century Christians to go *everywhere preaching the word*[Ac.8:1,4] throughout their known world, and far beyond, as Christ had told them to do.[Ac.1:8] This included *Parthians, and Medes, and Elamites, and the dwellers in Mesopotamia, and in Judaea, and Cappadocia, Pontus, and Asia, Phrygia, and Pamphylia, Egypt, and the parts of Libya about Cyrene, and Rome, Jews and proselytes, Cretes and Arabians.*[Ac.2:9-11]

Those early believers were determined to carry Christ's message to the *uttermost part of the world.*[Ac.1:8] Paul spoke of pressing on to the western edge of the continent: *When I take my journey into Spain.*[Ro.15:24]

Reliable Church historians concur that those early believers who were *scattered abroad*[Ac.8:1,4] proclaimed the gospel and established churches all across northern Africa.

Other sources and legends give reports of them spreading Christ's message toward the north and the west of Europe, penetrating numerous kingdoms in regions that we now know as Great Britain and Scandinavia.

Subjugated By Theocracy

But what happened? The ecclesiastical hierarchy gradually dominated Christianity and suffocated the idea of reaching *heathen* nations. The believers were finally subjugated by the State theocracy.

As Church dogmas superseded personal faith in Christ, the salvation of God became a *status conferred by the authority of ecclesiastics.* The government and the church became one. Registration (through baptism) as a member of *official* Christianity became a prominent part of respected citizenship.

The concept of winning *un*converted people was lost because society was already identified with the church which had become the authority for legitimizing births, education, marriages, employment, social activities, deaths, burials and the destinies of souls. To the official Church, peoples of *inferior* nations were no more than potential slaves, and the passion to reach them with the gospel was extinguished.

Political *Missions*

Taking the gospel to other nations, as Christ commanded, became a political ploy in the State theocracy. Pretending to be *representatives of Christ*, pontiffs sent envoys to foreign lands, but their interest was not to preach the gospel; their strategy was to establish or embellish political liaisons for the empire.

There was Ulphilas's mission to the Goths in 342, St. Patrick's mission to Ireland in 432, Columba's mission to Iona (Inner Hebrides) in 563, Boniface's mission to the Germans in 716, Cyril and Methodius' mission to the Slavs in 862, missions into Russia in 988 and into South and North America in later years, Xavier's mission to India in 1552, to Japan in 1549, and Ricci and Ruggieri's mission to China in 1582.

These were predominantly church sponsored trade missions in the interest of strengthening the broad political influence of the official Church.

The Renewed Dream
The Regions Beyond

As the *Reformation* inspired by Luther broke the spiritual siege of the long Dark Ages, Christians were no longer subjugated by the dictums of medieval ecclesiasticism. They began to dream again of carrying Christ's message of truth and salvation to the *regions beyond*.

The first Moravian missionaries from Saxony (East Germany, around Dresden) went abroad in 1732 to teach the gospel among the black slaves in the West Indies, and soon established missions in Greenland, Surinam, South Africa, Algiers, and among the North American Indians.

In the late seventeen hundreds God raised up William Carey who, like Paul, was consumed with a passion to share the gospel with *heathen* nations because he contended that all peoples of all ethnic groups have the same spiritual value in God's eyes, that they are all created by Him and that they all deserve to know about His love.

Rediscovering Missions

There was no church sponsored political motivation behind Carey's concern for these *heathen* and *pagan* peoples. His proposition was that while governments were trading with these nations, the church should be sharing the gospel with them.

Slave traders were trafficking in hundreds of thousands of human lives. Carey believed that they all had souls and were valuable to God; that Christians must give them the gospel and lead them to faith in Christ. He wrote what became a renowned pamphlet entitled, *An Enquiry into the Obligation of Christians to Use Means for the Conversion of the Heathens*. That pamphlet promoted new thinking in the Church.

Working as a shoe cobbler in England, William Carey dreamed of new ideas. He envisioned instituting medical and educational services in these nations.

He translated the entire Bible into the complex languages of Bengali, Oriya, Marathi, Hindi, Assamese, and Sanskrit, and portions of it into twenty-nine other languages. He edited and prepared grammars in seven languages and dictionaries in Bengali, Sanskrit, and Marathi, plus publishing two major works on horticulture.

Carey contended that those steps, combined with medical services, would not only advance those nations, but would open the way for teaching them the gospel. Those activities came to be known as *missions*.

New Societies—New Organizations

The Christian Church grasped Carey's new *missions* concepts and rapidly inaugurated church boards and missionary associations to spread the message of Christ worldwide.

In 1810 the *American Board of Commissioners for Foreign Missions* was formed.

In 1816 Adoniram Judson and his wife, Ann Hasseltine sailed for Burma where they translated the Bible into Burmese and wrote a full Burmese dictionary that is today's standard. They founded a church, established schools and trained national preachers, combining their translation and literary work with evangelism.

In 1840 David Livingstone sailed for Africa as a missionary and explorer. He soon became convinced that African converts were well able to share their Christian faith without the intervention of white officialdom in the mission. He was noted for his confidence in *spreading the gospel through "native agents"* as they were called.

In 1866 Hudson Taylor formed the *China Inland Mission*.

The *missionary* vision that had been lost during the Dark Ages, had at last regained prominence in the Church of Jesus Christ. Christians once again realized the value of human persons, regardless of their skin color, gender or nationality.

Church organizations began forming *Missionary Boards* and sponsoring men and women as *missionaries* to *non*-Christian nations. Bible schools and training institutions were inaugurated. Tens of thousands of men and women began to commit their lives to sharing Christ and His gospel in *heathen* lands and among *pagan* peoples as they were called then. As a result, multiplied millions have believed the gospel and thousands of them have become teachers, preachers and pastors.

Some of the largest Christian organizations and *the* largest churches in the world flourish in what the *Caucasian* world has referred to as *heathen* and *pagan* nations. (Part of chapter 15 shares information about *The World's New Missionaries* who are coming, by the thousands, from nations which have been demeaningly labeled the "third" world.)

The Church—One Body

Today, the Church of Jesus Christ is ONE BODY. *There is one body, and one Spirit, even as you are called in one hope of your calling; one Lord, one faith, one baptism, one God and Father of all, who is above all, and through all, and in you all. And unto every one is given grace according to the measure of the gift of Christ...*

And he gave some apostles; and some, prophets; and some, evangelists; and some, pastors and teachers; for

the perfecting of the saints, for the work of the minis-
try, for the edifying of the body of Christ: until we all
come into the unity of the faith, and of the knowledge
of the Son of God, unto a perfect person, unto the
measure of the stature of the fulness of Christ.[Ep.4:4-7,11-13]

✧ ✧ ✧

UNTIL RECENT DECADES, this sweeping renaissance of missions to what was called *heathen*
nations, though successful, had not included the
element of signs and miracles which distinguished First Century believers. We shall look
now at the recovery of this essential truth which
was so vital in witnessing for Christ during the
First Century.

Chapter 21

Miracles, Signs And Wonders

THE SUPERNATURAL POWER of God that confirmed the ministry of First Century believers, is another quality of early Christianity that was obliterated during the Dark Ages. Except for rare cases, God's miracle power did not regain its rightful place in gospel ministry until the turn of the 20th Century. The Bible says, *Jesus of Nazareth was approved by miracles and wonders and signs, which God did by him.*^{Ac.2:22} Without miraculous validation of the good news, Christianity cannot be proven to be more than another religion.

BEING BORN AGAIN IS A MIRACLE!

Everywhere that Jesus preached and taught, *many believed in his name, when they saw the miracles which he did.*^{Jn.2:23} *God anointed Jesus of Nazareth with the Holy Spirit and with power: who went about doing good, and healing all that were oppressed of the devil; for God was with him.*^{Ac.10:38}

Mark records that after Jesus was taken up into heaven, following His resurrection, His followers *went forth, and preached every where, the Lord work-*

298

*ing with them, and confirming the word with signs following.*Mk.16:20

The writer of Hebrews says that *this great salvation was first spoken by the Lord, then was confirmed unto us by them that heard him; God also bearing them witness, both with signs and wonders, and with divers miracles, and gifts of the Holy Spirit.*He.2:3-4 Paul recounts that through his ministry, *Christ wrought mighty signs and wonders, by the power of the Spirit of God; by which the Gentiles were made obedient to the gospel by word and deed.*Ro.15:18-19

First Century Christians fully expected that when they witnessed of Christ's resurrection and proclaimed His gospel, God would perform signs and miracles by the power of the Holy Spirit to confirm their message.

Over Fourteen Centuries
Without The Miraculous

But as the early church gained in political influence and popularity, they waned in spiritual power. Miracles were no longer considered vital to their ministry.

The supernatural was so completely extinguished from public worship and Christian teaching that many historical churches in our century believe and teach that when the apostles died, miracles ceased.

It is hard to realize that supernatural signs and physical miracles were largely absent in Christianity for almost fifteen centuries.

20th Century Rediscovery

It was not until around the turn of the 20th Century that a new awakening concerning the miracle working power of the Holy Spirit was experienced among Christians in various parts of the world.

Supernatural experiences were reported in Russia, Canada, the United States, Chile, South America, (and no doubt in other places), concerning Christians and church leaders who were receiving the apostolic baptism of the Holy Spirit.

In 1944, a 75 year old Methodist preacher attended Montavilla Tabernacle, the church that we pastored in Portland, Oregon. He told us that in 1895, he was praying with a group of Methodists in West Virginia. This is what he said took place:

"As we prayed to God, suddenly a wind was felt blowing through the room where we were gathered. In amazement, we noticed blazes of fire dancing upon the heads of those who prayed. We were overwhelmed by the ecstasy of the event and found ourselves praising God in strange languages that none of us understood. We realized that we were being baptized in the Holy Spirit in the same way that Christ's followers were baptized on the day of Pentecost, and we were astounded. "

These powerful outpourings were being accompanied by miracles, signs and wonders. Gifts of the Spirit, as expressed by Paul to the Corinthian believers, began to be exercised, including a rediscovery of Christ's power to heal the sick and to perform miracles.[Ro.15:18-19, He.2:3-4]

Miracles And Healings
The Key To Success

The director of a coalition of 28 Christian church organizations in India reports that their success in planting over *500 churches per month* is largely due to supernatural healings and miracles which they say is positive proof of God's presence and blessing on the people.

Daisy and I are living witnesses of the power and effectiveness of preaching the gospel *with signs following.* We have done that together in seventy-three nations, among the peoples of most of the major *non*-Christian religions of the world, during well over a half century. (See chapter 16) Since my wife's demise, I have continued in this ministry to many additional nations.

New Testament Ministry

IN TESTIMONY OF the gospel which Christ told His followers to proclaim to the world, I have arranged here a compendium of Bible quotations for the encouragement of Christian leaders and lay persons who believe that Jesus Christ is unchanged today.

We give our witness that *all that Jesus began both to do and teach until the day in which he was taken up* Ac.1:1-2 is still God's will for today. We are convinced that *all the promises of God in him are yes and amen,*2Co.1:20 and that they *are for you, and for your children, and for all that are afar off, even as many as the Lord our God shall call.*Ac.2:39

*The glorious gospel of the blessed God, has been committed to our trust.*1Ti.1:11 Our message is that *Christ Jesus came into the world to save sinners.*1Ti.1:15

*For Christ's death on the cross has made peace with God for us all by His blood.*Col.1:20LB *He has brought us back as his friend, and has done this through the death on the cross of his own human body, and now as a result, we [as believers] are standing before God with nothing left against us, the only condition being that we fully believe the truth, convinced of the good news that Jesus died for us.*Col.1:28-29LB

For Christ sent us to preach the gospel: not with wisdom of words, lest the cross of Christ should be

made of none effect. *For the preaching of the cross is to them that perish foolishness; but to us which are saved, it is the power of God.*[1Co.1:17-18]

We believe that *God, who at various times and in different ways spoke in time past to the fathers by the prophets, has in these last days spoken to us by his Son*[He.1:1-2] *whom he anointed with the Holy Ghost and with power: who went about doing good, and healing all that were oppressed of the devil.*[Ac.10:38]

This *Jesus of Nazareth was a man approved of God among people by miracles and wonders and signs which God did by him.*[Ac.2:22] And He promised, *Lo, I am with you alway, even unto the end of the world.*[Mt.28:20] *I will never leave you nor forsake you.*[He.13:5]

Christ has clearly said: *If we believe on him, the works that he does, we shall do also...and whatever we shall ask in his name, he will do, that the Father may be glorified in the Son.*[Jn.14:12-13]

So, *this is the confidence that we have in him that if we ask anything according to God's will* [or Word of promise], *he hears us: and if we know that he hears us, whatever we ask, we know that we have the petitions that we desire of him.*[1Jn.5:14-15]

We walk by faith, and not by sight,[2Co.5:7] knowing that *without faith, it is impossible to please God;*[He.11:6] that *the just shall live by faith.*[Ro.1:17]

As *great multitudes come together to hear, and to be healed by Christ of their infirmities,*Lu.5:15 we know that *faith can only come to them by hearing, and hearing by the word of God.*Ro.10:17 So we constantly *teach and preach the gospel of the kingdom,*Mt.4:23 because Jesus said, *if I be lifted up, I will draw all people to me.*Jn.12:32 *For other foundation can no one lay than that is laid, which is Jesus Christ.*1Co.3:11

Whenever we enter a city, we *speak boldly in the name of the Lord, who gives testimony to the word of his grace, and grants signs and wonders to be done.*Ac.14:3 *The hand of the Lord is with us: and great numbers believe, and turn to the Lord.*Ac.11:21

As we *preach Christ* [to them], *the people with one accord give heed to the thing which we speak, hearing and seeing the miracles which are done, and there is great joy in each city.*Ac.8:6-8 Many times *unbelievers say, What shall we do? For that indeed a notable miracle has been done is manifest to all that dwell in the city, and we cannot deny it.*Ac.4:16 *Many of them that hear the word believe: and the number of them is* [usually] *thousands.*Ac.4:4 *Believers are the more added to the Lord, multitudes both of men and women,*Ac.5:14 [and they] *glorify God for what is done.*Ac.4:21

Those who are healed are told to *go home to their friends, and to tell how great things the Lord has done for them, and has had compassion on them. And they publish in their areas how great things Jesus has done for them: and the people marvel.*Mk.5:19-20

We come not to the people with excellency of speech or of wisdom, and we determine to know nothing among them, save Jesus Christ and him crucified. Our speech and our preaching is not with enticing words of human wisdom, but in demonstration of the Spirit and of power. [We teach] that one's faith should not stand in the wisdom of people but in the power of God.[1Co.2:1-5]

We declare the gospel by which people are saved, how that Christ died for our sins according to the scriptures; and that he was buried, and that he rose again the third day.[1Co.15:1-4] [We believe this is vital because] if Christ be not risen, then is our preaching vain, and our faith is vain, and we are false witnesses of Christ.[1Co.15:13-15]

And since the bible says, faith comes by hearing the word of God,[Ro.10:17] how shall people hear without a preacher?[Ro.10:14] [That is why] we are ready to preach the gospel,[Ro.1:15] and we are not ashamed of the Gospel,[Ro.1:16] and we declare the gospel.[1Co.15:1]

[We believe that] after people hear the word of truth, the gospel of salvation, [they are] sealed with the holy Spirit of promise,[Ep.1:13] [and they become] partakers of the promise in Christ by the gospel, whereof we are made ministers, according to the gift of the grace of God given to us by the effectual working of his power. To us is this grace given, that we should preach among the Gentiles [non-Christians] the unsearchable riches of Christ.[Ep.3:6-9]

[We consider that] *we have been allowed of God to be put in trust with the gospel, and so we speak it; not as pleasing people, but God.*[1Th.2:4]

[We know that] *if anyone is in Christ, he or she is a new creature: old things are passed away, behold all thing are become new.*[2Co.5:17]

[We] *declare before all the people* [Lu.8:47] *that in Christ alone is life;*[Jn.1:4] *that God has given to us eternal life, and that this life is in his Son. Whoever has the Son has life; and whoever has not the Son of God has not life.*[1Jn.5:11-12] *As many as receive Jesus Christ, to them he gives power to become the children of God.*[Jn.1:12]

[We say]: *These things have we spoken to you that you may know that you have eternal life, and that you may believe on the name of the Son of God,*[1Jn.5:11-13] because *there is no other name under heaven given among us, by which we may be saved.*[Ac.4:12] *And with many other words do we testify and exhort, saying,* [Ac.2:40] *whosoever shall call on the name of the Lord shall be saved.*[Ro.10:13] [And thank God,] *believers are the more added to the Lord, multitudes both of men and women.*[Ac.5:14]

The word of God increases; and the number of disciples multiplies greatly; and a great company of [**non-Christian religions**] *are obedient to the faith,*[Ac.6:7] *so mightily grows the word of God and prevails.*[Ac.19:20] *Also the name of the Lord Jesus is magnified.*[Ac.19:17]

[We emphasize that] *God is not a man, that he should lie; neither the son of man, that he should repent: If he has said it, he will do it. If he has spoken, he will make it good,*[Nu.23:19] [because He has said], *I am the Lord: I will speak, and the word that I shall speak shall come to pass; I will say the word, and will perform it.*[Ez.12:25] [He says,] *the word which I have spoken shall be done.*[Ez.12:28] *The Lord will do the thing that he has promised.*[Is.38:7] [He says,] *Yes, I have spoken it, and I will also bring it to pass; I have purposed it, and I will also do it.*[Is.46:11] [We assure the people that] *heaven and earth shall pass away, but Christ's words shall not pass away.*[Mt.24:35]

[We always emphasize that since] *now is the accepted time, and now is the day of salvation,*[2Co.6:2] anyone can *repent and be converted, and your sins will be blotted out* [Ac.3:19] *by looking to Jesus the author and finisher of your faith* [He.12:2] *who has redeemed you to God,*[Re.5:9] [because] *he loved you and washed you from your sins in his own blood* [Re.1:5] *of the new testament, which is shed for many for the remission of sins.*[Mt.26:28]

[So we encourage people to] *reckon yourself dead indeed to sin, but alive to God through Jesus Christ your Lord...for the wages of sin is death; but the gift of God is eternal life through Jesus Christ our Lord.*
[Ro.6:11,23]

May these verses encourage faith in the gospel.

◇ ◇ ◇

WE HAVE NOW REVIEWED some of the truths and dynamic methods of First Century Christians, methods and truths which were extinguished during the Dark Ages, but which have regained prominence in the Church today.

Now we shall look at *the master key to the unprecedented success of Early Church believers* – their passion to witness to individuals whenever and wherever they could engage them in conversation.

Chapter 22

Witnesses Of Christ

PERSONAL EVANGELISM, witnessing to individuals out wherever they can be encountered,
was a normal practice of First Century Christians.
But the idea was obliterated during the Dark
Ages and has only regained *prominence* in recent
decades. Think of it!

Followers of Christ considered themselves to
be, above all else, **His witnesses**. He had told
them, *You shall receive power after that the Holy
Ghost is come upon you: and **you shall be witnesses
unto me**...*[Ac.1:8] So they said, *This Jesus has God
raised up, whereof **we all are witnesses**.*[Ac.2:32] *And he
was seen many days of them...**who are his witnesses
unto the people**.*[Ac.13:30-31] See also Ac.1:22;4:33;10:39;10:42;23:11;26:16;
He.12:1; Re.20:4

Why were they *witnesses* of Christ? Because He
had come as the savior and redeemer of humanity. But Jewish Rabbis did not believe on Him,
therefore they never taught the people that He

was the *One* sent from God as their Messiah and redeemer?

Was Jesus The Messiah?

The supernatural events surrounding Jesus Christ's birth, life, ministry, death, burial, resurrection and ascension *identified Him as the Messianic savior whom Bible prophets said would come.*[Is.7:14; 9:6-7]

Those who had heard Him and had seen His miracles, believed on Him and became His followers.[Jn.2:23;6:2] But religious rulers considered it heresy to believe that this Jesus was the *One* spoken of by their prophets.

Jesus constantly showed that the scriptures bore witness of Him. *Beginning at Moses and all the prophets, he expounded unto them in all the scriptures the things **concerning himself**.*[Lu.24:27] He said, *While I was with you, I spoke of all the things that must be fulfilled, which were written in the law of Moses, and in the prophets, and in the psalms, **concerning me**.*[Lu.24:44]

He told the Jews who claimed to know and believe the Old Testament, to *search the scriptures; for* [He said], *they testify **of me**.*[Jn.5:39] And He added, *If you had believed Moses* [as you pretend to], *you would have believed me: for he wrote **of me**.*[Jn.5:46]

Great controversy surrounded Christ's ministry. He came as *the Prince of Peace*.[Is.9:6] People had never received that peace through religion.

Crucifixion—Resurrection

Peace with God and the joy that believers in the Lord Jesus discovered, was such that they wanted to help others experience it. They perceived the fulfillment of prophecies in everything that Christ said and did.

Those who rejected Him were blind to His prophetic fulfillment, and believed that His teachings were deceitful [Mt.27:63; Jn.7:12] and that His miracles were wrought by the power of Beelzebub.[Mt.9:34;12:24; Mk.3:22]

Rabbinical opposition finally succeeded in bringing about the crucifixion of Christ.[Mt.27:31; Mk.15:13-14; Jn.19:6] It was presumed that His influence was ended. Most of His followers had been scattered,[Jn.21:3; Mt.26:56; Mk.14:15; Lu.24:13-21] but some women believers stayed by His tomb and He appeared to them.[Mt.28:1-10; Mk.16:1-8; Jn.20:11-17]

Those women went and told the disciples that Jesus was alive.[Lu.24:9-11; Jn.20:18] Then He revealed Himself to them also.[Mt.28:18; Mk.16:12-14; Lu.24:15-31; Jn.20:19-29] *He showed himself alive...by many infallible proofs, being seen of them forty days, and speaking of the things pertaining to the kingdom of God.*[Ac.1:3]

Many of Christ's early followers were living *witnesses* of His life, death, burial and resurrection. Since this Jesus was the *One* spoken of in the books of Moses, the prophets, and the Psalms, Lu.24:27,44; Jn.1:45; Ac.26:22-23;28:23 they believed that everyone should be told about Him because prophets had said, *whoever called on his name would be delivered.* Jl.2:32

This was the *good tidings* Is.52:2;61:1-2; Lu.2:10 which every Jew had waited for. Those who had found this spiritual deliverance and peace were willing to lay down their lives to *witness* of Christ to others.

Miracle Confirmation

AN ANGEL APPEARED when Jesus was born, saying, *Behold, I bring you good tidings of great joy...to all people. For unto you is born a savior, which is Christ the Lord.*Lu.2:10-11 This was the greatest news and it brought greater hope than the people had ever tasted before.

Another visitation occurred. At the temple, the priest, Zacharias, had received a great miracle healing from God Lu.1:18-22,59-64 and *was filled with the Holy Ghost, and prophesied.*Lu.1:67 Under this new power, he spoke about this savior and deliverer and *his sayings were noised abroad throughout all the* *hill country of Judea and all that heard them laid them up in their hearts.*[Lu.1:65-66]

Zacharias spoke these words as an oracle of God: *The Lord has visited and redeemed his people...as he spoke by the mouth of his prophets...that we should be delivered out of the hand of our enemies and serve God without fear, in holiness and righteousness...he has given knowledge of salvation by the remission of sins...and will guide our feet in the way of peace.*[Lu.1:68-79]

The Promise of Peace

Such peace was unknown among the Hebrew people. Religion for them was exacting, severe, legalistic, and without compassion. Prophets had spoken of a savior who would bring peace and salvation. Every Jew longed for this redeemer. Now this man called Jesus from Nazareth had come. Everything about Him was a fulfillment of prophecies. Those who believed on Him experienced life-changing miracles and peace which had not been known before.

Light had come to the *Gentiles* [the *"nations"*, the non-Jews].[Is.42:6;60:3; Lu.2:32; Ac.13:47] Those who believed on Jesus as their Lord, wanted people to know that this man was the Christ, the savior who had been spoken of by the prophets and who would bring *peace* to the people.

He was *the word which God sent unto the* [world], *preaching **peace** by Jesus Christ.*^{Ac.10:36}

People Telling People

There was a strange prophet preaching in the wilderness called John the Baptist, *bearing witness of Christ, and he cried, saying, This is he of whom I spoke…No one has seen God* [but] *this only begotten Son…has declared* [revealed] *him…Behold he is the Lamb of God, that takes away the sin of the world.*^{Jn.1:15-18,29}

John was one of those early *witnesses. He bare record* [witnessed]; *I saw the Spirit descending from heaven like a dove, and it abode upon him.* [God told me] *Upon whom you see the Spirit descending, and remaining, the same is he…and I saw, and do bare record that this is the Son of God.*^{Jn.1:32-34}

The next day, while John was speaking about Christ, two of his friends looked and saw Jesus and were convinced that He was the *One* of whom the prophets had spoken. *They followed Jesus,*^{Jn.1:35-37} and went to tell others about Him. One of them *found his brother, Simon, and said to him, We have found the Messiah, which is, being interpreted, the Christ. And he brought him to Jesus.*^{Jn.1:40-42}

The following day, a man named Philip followed the Lord, then he *found Nathanael, and said to him, We have found him, of whom Moses in the law, and the prophets, did write, Jesus of Nazareth.*^{Jn.1:43-45}

Jesus began doing *miracles, manifesting forth his glory; and his disciples believed on him.*Jn.2:11 People saw Him, heard Him and believed on Him as their savior and Lord. They began following Him and telling others about Him. *Many believed in his name, when they saw the miracles which he did.*Jn.2:23

Christ For All Races

The yearning to know when this Messiah would come, preoccupied all kinds of people. Jesus met and conversed with a Samaritan woman at a public well, which was highly unusual because the *Jews have no dealings with Samaritans.*Jn.4:9 Also, rabbinical law strictly forbade any male Jew to speak with a woman in public.

When Jesus discerned details about the woman's private life, she said, *Sir, I perceive that you are a prophet...I know that when Messiah comes, which is called Christ: he will tell us all things.*Jn.4:19,25

Jesus revealed Himself to that Samaritan woman Jn.4:26 and the first thing she did was to *leave her water pot, go into the city, and tell the people, Come, see a man, which told me all things that I ever did: is not this the Christ?* Jn.4:28-29 Then [the people] *went out of the city, and came unto him...and many of the Samaritans believed on him for the saying of the woman...and many more believed because of his own word.*Jn.4:39,41

His Fame Spread Abroad

As soon as people believed on Jesus, they began to tell others about Him. They became His *witnesses*.

And his fame spread through all Syria; and they brought unto him all sick people that were taken with divers diseases and torments, and those who were possessed with devils, and those who were lunatic, and those who had palsy; and he healed them. And there followed him great multitudes of people.[Mt.4:24-25] *They spread abroad his fame in all the country.*[Mt.9:31]

Needy people heard about Him, came to Him and were blessed. Then they went out and told others about Him until *wherever He went, in villages, or cities, or the country, they laid the sick in the streets, and besought him that they might touch if it were but the border of his garment: and as many as touched him were made whole.*[Mk.6:56]

Multitudes followed Him and as they believed on Him, He taught them truths that Rabbis in the synagogues or temples had never spoken of. The most revolutionary concept that He introduced was about *God being His Father, making Himself God's Son.*[Jn.5:17-18;6:57;14:9-11] (See chapter 4) This was so offensive to the Jews that it finally precipitated His crucifixion.[Jn.19:7]

Witnessing—Confessing

ONCE THE PUBLIC crucifixion of this man from Nazareth had been performed, the Jewish rulers thought His influence would dissipate. But three days later, the most crucial news of all was reported. Women found the tomb of Jesus empty. They said that angels had appeared at the sepulchre announcing that Christ had risen from the dead.Lu.24:1-6 They even said that Jesus Himself had appeared to them.Mt.28:9-10; Jn.20:14-17

This news quickly reached the chief priests who *took counsel and gave large money unto the soldiers, instructing them, Say that his disciples came by night, and stole him away while we slept. And if this come to the governor's ears, we will persuade him, and secure you. So the soldiers took the money, and did as they were told: and this saying is commonly reported among the Jews until this day.*Mt.28:12-15

But Jesus *showed himself alive by many infallible proofs.*Ac.1:3 He appeared to two disciples as they walked along a roadway,Lu.24:13-32 to the eleven disciples behind closed doors,Jn.20:19-23; 26-29; Mk.16:14-18; Lu.24:36-52 to some of His followers who had returned to their fishing nets after He had been crucified,Jn.21:1-14 to those who witnessed His ascension,Lu.24:50 to Peter,1Co.15:5 to five hundred of His followers at one time,1Co.15:6 to James,1Co.15:7 to Paul at his conversion,Ac.9:5; 1Co.15:8 and we have no way of knowing how many more times He appeared to them.[Ac.1:3] We do know that He made these appearances during a period of forty days.[Ac.1:3]

Incontrovertible Proof

These many *infallible*[Ac.1:3] appearances, after He had been publicly crucified, were incontrovertible proof to His followers that He was the Messiah of whom Moses and the prophets had spoken and whom God had raised from the dead according to the scriptures.

First Century believers considered that after they embraced Jesus as *The Christ, The One* spoken of by the prophets, their mission was to communicate that revelation to as many others as they could engage.

A description of Paul's ministry in *The Acts* states that his *manner was to reason with people out of the scriptures, explaining and proving that it was necessary for Christ to suffer and to rise from the dead, saying that this Jesus whom I preach unto you is Christ* [the anointed One, the Messiah].[Ac.17:2-3KJV & NRSV] The record states that *he preached unto them Jesus, and the resurrection.*[Ac.17:18] That was the *witness* or the *confession* that Early Church believers gave of Him to people.

The Sign Of His Return

This is why they grasped Christ's words about receiving power to be His *witnesses...unto the uttermost part of the earth.*[Ac.1:8] He had told them that *this gospel should be preached in all the world for a witness to all nations; and **then** the end would come.* [Mt.24:14] He had said this when they asked: *What shall be **the** sign of your coming, and of the end of the world?* [Mt.24:3]

Those First Century Christians believed that the Messiah, *the One* announced by their prophets, had come. They had recognized Him and had become His followers.

Early followers of Christ believed that He had come to show the world what God is like in a human person — *in flesh.*[Jn.1:14] *God was in Christ, reconciling the world unto himself.*[2Co.5:19] *He had come down from heaven not to do his own will, but the will of the Father who had sent him.*[Jn.6:38] *The Word was made flesh, and dwelt among them, (and they beheld his glory, the glory as of the only begotten of the Father,) full of grace and truth.*[Jn.1:14] *No one had seen God at any time; but the only begotten Son, he declared him.*[Jn.1:18]

Confessing And Witnessing

Christ had told these First Century followers exactly what to do. *Whoever will confess me before* *people, I will confess them before my Father in heaven.*Mt.10:32; Lu.12:8 To *witness* of Christ and to *confess* Him before people became their life's passion because as soon as they could tell everyone about Him, He had promised to return.Mt.24:14; 26:64; Lu.21:27; Ac.1:8-11; He.9:28

Later, Paul emphasized that witnessing and confessing of Christ is the proof of faith for salvation. *If you will confess with your mouth the Lord Jesus, and believe in your heart that God has raised him from the dead, you will be saved.*Ro.10:9

Jesus had told them: The Holy Spirit *shall testify of me: And you also shall bear witness of me, because you have been with me from the beginning.*Jn.16:27 Their mission was to *witness* and *confess* Christ to people. That was what the Holy Spirit had come upon them to do.

Peter said, *This Jesus has God raised up, whereof we are witnesses.*Ac.2:32 Later, the record states: *And with great power gave the apostles witness of the resurrection of the Lord Jesus.*Ac.4:33

Miracles And Multitudes

Peter and John found a crippled beggar and witnessed to him about Christ, prayed for him in the name of Jesus, lifted him on his feet, and the man was healed.Ac.3 A multitude gathered, curious about the prayer that they had prayed *in the name of a man whom they thought was dead.* How could a dead man bring about such a miracle? Their curiosity opened the door for Peter to give witness of Christ publicly, and it was the beginning of the believers good news message that Christ was risen from the dead.

The Witness of Stephen

Stephen, an ordinary layman gave a phenomenal witness of who this Jesus is, rehearsing scriptures from the books of Moses, the Psalms and the prophets which he said pointed to this Jesus. He even saw the fulfillment of prophecies in the way the Jewish leaders had become *the betrayers and murderers* of Jesus.[Ac.7:51-52] *When they heard these things, they were cut to the heart, and they gnashed on him with their teeth.*[Ac.7:54]

Their fury incited them to violence. Stephen *looked up steadfastly into heaven, and saw the glory of God, and Jesus standing on the right hand of God, and said, Behold I see the heavens opened, and the Son of man standing on the right hand of God.*[Ac.7:55-56]

For Stephen to pretend that he could see Jesus, this man thought to be an *impostor* and a *deceiver,* standing at God's right hand, was an intolerable insult to those who were persecuting Christ's followers.[Ac.7:55-59]

They cried out with a loud voice, and stopped their ears, and ran upon him with one accord, and cast him out of the city, and stoned him...calling on God, and saying, Lord Jesus, receive my spirit, and he kneeled down, and cried with a loud voice, Lord, lay not this sin to their charge. And when he had said this, he fell asleep.[Ac.7:57-60]

Great Persecution

The result of these powerful witnesses of Christ angered the Jews. *There was at that time great persecution against the believers...and they were all scattered abroad throughout the regions of Judea and Samaria...and they went everywhere preaching the word.*[Ac.8:1,4]

They were witnessing about Jesus Christ; throughout Asia, across the Roman Empire, then across northern Africa, westward to Spain, northward to the great kingdoms known today as Great Britain and Scandinavia, to the territories around the Black Sea, eastward across Persia, into Afghanistan and on to the south of India—and no one knows where else they carried the gospel.

⬦ ⬦ ⬦

BUT AS MORE converts were made—even among government officials,[Ph.4:22] they became so effective in their personal witnessing that they penetrated even the households of officialdom, which we shall discuss in the next chapter.

Chapter 23

The Emperor—The Monk

CHRISTIANS PAID TERRIBLE prices for their testimony of Christ during those first 300 years. Believers were accused, arrested, imprisoned, tortured, and martyred for their faith, particularly under the cruel reigns of Emperors Diocletian and Galerius. But their ruthless *Great Persecution* failed to silence the testimony of faith in Jesus Christ.

The Pivotal Event

Then something happened which the Christians believed to be the greatest triumph for Christ that they had ever known, *but which would eventually precipitate their spiritual suffocation* and would influence the affairs of Church and State for centuries to come.

What was this historical event? It was the conversion to Christianity of the Emperor Constantine *The Great*.

At the time of his conversion, there were two Roman Emperors. Constantine ruled the West of the Empire and Licinius, the East. Soon after Constantine's conversion, these two Emperors held a historic summit in the northern Italian city of Milan in January 313.

Edict of Milan

Out of this crucial conference to bring greater peace and harmony to the Empire, the rulers issued their salient *Edict of Milan* in which their joint-communiqué *granted full religious freedom for Roman citizens to become Christians, and restored all properties to Christians which had been confiscated by the state during the Great Persecution.*

This imperial decree set followers of Christ on a par with followers of any other religion, and *ended the Roman Empire's official persecution of Christians*. The age of the martyrs was closed and the transition to the *Christian Empire* began.

As Emperor, Constantine believed that he was God's chosen servant, responsible for the good government of his church. Though Christianity had been a minority sect, his imperial patronage caused it to become the official religion of the empire, and an indication of loyal citizenship. It was so popularized that many pagan temples were closed and even destroyed.

The Church and the Empire were regarded as *synonymous*. Before the end of the Fourth Century, Christianity had become *the only official religion of the Roman Empire*.

Imperial Patronage
And Spiritual Suffocation

But this Constantinian patronage and the resulting popularity of the Christian faith eventually engulfed the church in spiritual suffocation and, according to Church history, precipitated the tragic *spiritual decline* of First Century Christianity.

During this epoch, the church grew in wealth, in numbers, and in political and ecclesiastical domination. As the business world and general citizenry embraced the popularized *faith of the Emperor*, the soulwinning passion that had driven early believers, was extinguished. Christianity had become not only *official*, but *imperious* and *autocratic*. The power of the Holy Spirit had become nothing more than a doctrine, and worship had been reduced to a ritual.

Ecclesiastical dicta and dogmas had replaced personal knowledge of Christ, and the passion to *confess* Him and to *witness* of Him to the *unconverted* no longer burned in the hearts of Church members. Ecclesiastical favor strangled the spiritual life of believers and a thousand years of pontifical domination ensued.

New Beginnings

THEN REVELATION CAME to an obscure monk in the early 1500s that started the gradual rediscovery of truths and methods which had distinguished First Century believers, but which had been smothered during the Dark Ages.

The first such rediscovery was that *faith did not consist of assenting to the dogmas of ecclesiasticism, but consisted of each person trusting the promises of God and the merits of Christ for his or her own salvation.*

This revelation came to a religious friar named Martin Luther as he pondered the abusive sale of *indulgences* by the church to raise funds to finance favored projects approved by the hierarchy.

Indulgences were documents prepared by the church and sold by priests to individuals either for themselves or on behalf of the dead. In return for money, the purchaser (or someone deceased) would be released from purgatory for a certain number of years.

Tetzel's Abuse of Indulgences

A German Dominican friar, Johann Tetzel, orchestrated the sale of these indulgences to excite public interest, crafting his sermons to delight and persuade people, often climaxing with his popularized lines: *Once the coin into the coffer clings, a soul from purgatory heaven-ward springs!*

This abusive practice by Tetzel drove Martin Luther to deeper study and to the conclusion that *salvation was not a commodity to be dispensed by ecclesiastical authority.* He concluded that *any person who would believe the scriptures could be saved by faith alone in God's love and grace, without acquiescence to the religious system.*

Luther's position contravened official Church doctrine to such a degree that ecclesiastical authorities judged it to be heretical and threatening to the autocratic ecclesiastical system.

On October 31, 1517, this 33-year-old monk nailed his 95 Thesis to the door of the Castle Church in Wittenberg, sounding the trumpet that Paul had sounded among First Century believers that *the just shall live by faith.*[Ro.1:17; Ga.3:11]

New Faith—New Discoveries

Christians began to read the scriptures for themselves and ecclesiastic imperialism of the Middle Ages began to lose its influence. *The renaissance of First Century Christian faith was under way.*

As a result of this new freedom, many new Christian societies and church organizations were instituted. New life was birthed in believers and the passion to witness to the unconverted was re-born.

New Age of *Reason*

But this long nightmare of church authoritarian-ism and hypocrisy had precipitated the new *Age of Reason*. Society had abandoned faith in God for scholasticism, humanism, atheism and the broad spectrum of secularized theories which were an-tagonistic to Christian doctrine.

Public religion skepticism alerted Christian leaders about the urgency for gospel promulga-tion *on a broad scale*. God began raising up great evangelists like Wesley, Whitfield and Finney. Mass evangelism that had shaken the Roman Empire in First Century Christianity, began to shake the new world as the influence of the gos-pel was matched against humanistic philoso-phies. These evangelism crusades influenced multitudes in the new world to embrace Christ in simple faith.

Unto The Uttermost Part

This sweep of biblical Christianity expanded the thinking of believers. American Indians began to be evangelized. Moravian missionaries set out to minister the gospel to slaves in the Caribbean area. God was restoring the original passion of

His followers to be *His witnesses unto the uttermost part of the earth.*^{Ac.1:8}

William Carey, a shoe cobbler in England, came to the realization that the people of *heathen* nations had souls and had the same value in God's sight as anyone else. He carried the Christian message to India and Burma, as Hudson Taylor did to China and as David Livingstone did to Africa.

The missionary vision of First Century Christianity was alive again. As Paul had penetrated Gentile areas throughout the Roman Empire, now Christians were reaching out to share Christ and His gospel with *heathen* and *pagan* peoples of the post Dark Age world.

Then another spiritual crisis was imminent.

Rediscovery Of The Supernatural

As the Church expanded into *non*-Christian nations where they were witnessing to peoples of *pagan* religions, the miraculous was needed to convince these people of the claims of the gospel, as much as it had been needed in Bible days.

As mentioned in Chapter 21, at the turn of the 20th Century, God's power began falling upon believers in a fresh, apostolic baptism of the Holy Spirit, with supernatural gifts (defined by Paul [1Co.12:1,4-11,27-31]), and with a renewed discovery of

Christ's power to heal the sick and to perform miracles.^{Ro.15:18-19; He.2:3-4}

This produced the same results as it did among First Century believers; *With great power they gave witness of the resurrection of the Lord Jesus: and great grace was upon them all,*^{Ac.4:33} *God bearing them witness, both with signs and wonders, and with divers miracles, and gifts of the Holy Ghost, according to his own will.*^{He.2:4}

The road back to God's spiritual fullness in the believers had been long and fraught with many obstacles. But clearly, the great truths embraced by early Christians were being rediscovered.

These events bore many and varied labels. In the mid 1700s, people called it the *campmeeting* epoch. In the 1800s, the *brush arbor* became popular. Next, *revival* became vogue, then the terms *revival* and *evangelism* became intermingled. Following that, evangelistic *crusades* or *campaigns*, either centered in churches or in auditoriums for city-wide efforts, became popular.

◇ ◇ ◇

As THE HOLY SPIRIT became active again among believers, Joel's prophecy which Peter quoted on the day of Pentecost, began to receive new attention. The Church began to realize that God had sent His Spirit upon *all flesh*, and that His plan for *the last days* was that His message be proclaimed by both His *sons and His daughters, by servants and by handmaidens alike.*[Ac.2:16-18]

In the next chapter we shall discuss real and profound meaning of this word *prophesy*, and who it applies to.

Chapter 24

Prophesy—Men & Women

CLEARLY, FOLLOWING THE great Reformation that Martin Luther led, powerful rediscoveries of First Century Christianity have been made: 1) Faith for salvation, 2) The gospel for all nations, 3) Mass evangelism, and 4) The miraculous confirmation of God's word. (Plus many others.)

But it is astounding that *the master key* to the success of Early Church believers would be among the last rediscoveries to be made by the Church of this century. *That key was, witnessing for Christ out where people live and work and play.* That concept made every First Century Christian vital in ministry—*the women the same as the men.*

I said it was *among* the last to be re-discovered because another redemptive truth which Christ taught, and which the Early Church embraced, but which has not yet been acclaimed, is *the issue of equality between Christian men and women.*

With The Women

When the Holy Spirit came upon those believers in Jerusalem, they *were in an upper room...in one accord, [and were] in prayer and supplication, with the women...*[Ac.1:13-14]

Equality of the sexes was a new distinction among the followers of Christ. *They were **all** filled with the Holy Ghost* [Ac.2:4] [both men and women — and for the same purpose — to be *witnesses* of Christ *to the uttermost part of the earth*]...and they **all** *spoke the wonderful works of God* [publicly].[Ac.2:11]

It was the season following the Passover, and people of many nationalities were in Jerusalem. When this supernatural event took place, the news spread rapidly and many people gathered to witness the unusual event.[Ac.2:6-12] They were amazed at the phenomenon, and said: *Are not all these that speak Galilaeans? How hear we everyone in our own tongue, wherein we were born?* [About sixteen different nationalities were named] [Ac.2:9-11]. *We hear them speak in our tongues **the wonderful works of God**. And they were all amazed...saying one to another, **What does this mean?*** [Ac.2:7-12]

It was truly remarkable — and significant that both the men and the women were publicly speaking *the wonderful works of God.*

Prophecy Fulfilled

Peter announced that it was the fulfillment of the Hebrew prophet, Joel's prophecy: *In the last days, saith God, I will pour out of my Spirit upon all flesh: and your **sons** and your **daughters** shall prophecy...*[Ac.2:14-17] And to further endorse both men and women *speaking the wonderful works of God,* he continued quoting from Joel: *And on my **servants** and on my **handmaidens** I will pour out in those days of my Spirit; **and they shall prophesy**.*[Ac.2:18]

What It Means To *Prophesy*

This word, *prophesy,* in its contemporary connotation expresses concepts forbidden to women in most churches. But this *female exclusion* is fostered by a wrong interpretation of the word, *prophesy.*

The 10 volume, 10,000 page *Kittel's Theological Dictionary of the New Testament* is considered the most respected and exhaustive authority among both Jewish and Christian biblical scholars in the world. Pages 781-861 of Vol.VI are given to elucidate the broad scope of the words, *prophesy* and *prophecy,* making it indelibly clear that the essence of both words applies to women in the Church, the same as to men. Here are excerpts from these pages:

> *Prophesy* or *prophecy* means: to proclaim, to declare openly, to make known publicly, as an oracle of God, His plan of salvation for the world

and His will for the life of Christians, including divine mysteries; to admonish the slothful and weary, to encourage those under assault, to speak with a sense of God-given authority and instruction to the Church. It is not addressed solely to Christians; it also has missionary significance…[to] lead non-Christians to recognition of their guilt and to worship God.

It is clear that the biblical meaning of these two words, *embraces the full scope of Christian Church ministry.* Christ's redemption has so totally ransomed, reconciled and restored humanity to God (*all* of humanity, both men and women equally) that *no ministry of the Church is off limits for women believers in the Body of Christ any more than it is for men believers.*

Prophesy—Both Men And Women

The apostle Paul urged all believers to *follow charity, and desire spiritual gifts, but **preferred that they prophesy.***[1Co.14:1] He repeated that he wished *all would speak with tongues, but **preferred that they prophesy.***[1Co.14:5] He stressed *that **all** may prophesy one by one, that all may learn and all may be comforted.*[1Co.14:31] He gave instruction to **men** when they prophesy,[1Co.11:4] then he gave instruction to **women** when they prophesy.[1Co.11:5]

It is self-evident that the terms, *prophesy* and *keep silence* [1Cor.14:34] are contradictory. Obviously there were legal or traditional or societal factors to be taken into account when Paul cautioned that women should *keep silence*.

Paul knew that Christ had empowered His followers, both men and women, to be His *witnesses ...unto the uttermost part of the earth,*[Ac.1:8] which women could not be if they *kept silence*.

Paul would not have carelessly countermanded His Lord in this matter unless the churches at Corinth and Ephesus were facing circumstances or persecution or danger or local traditions which were incompatible with Christ's commission.

Scattered Witnesses

Both men and women witnessed of Christ, *publicly and from house to house.*[Ac.20:20] They were both persecuted by opponents of the gospel. *Saul made havock of the church, entering into every house, and haling men **and women**, committed them to prison.*[Ac.8:3] That persecution scattered both men and women believers, and the record makes it clear that **all** who were scattered abroad *went everywhere preaching the Lord's message,*[Ac.8:4] something the women believers could not have done if they had *kept silent*. They were Christ's *witnesses*.

Jesus had said, *For the Son of man is come to seek and to save that which was lost.*[Lu.19:10] He had told His followers, *As my Father has sent me, even so send I you.*[Jn.20:21] And they had received a baptism of power from on high that gave them the same anointing that had rested upon their Lord, and for the same purpose.

Jesus had said, *The Spirit of the Lord is upon me, because he has anointed me to preach the gospel to the poor; he has sent me to heal the brokenhearted, to preach deliverance to the captives, and recovering of sight to the blind, to set at liberty them that are bruised, to preach the acceptable year of the Lord.*[Lu.4:18-19]

That same *Spirit of the Lord* had now come upon them, both the men and the women. *They were **all** filled with the Holy Ghost* [Ac.2:4] [for the same reason: *You shall be witnesses unto me*] [Ac.1:8], and they were **all** heard ***speaking the wonderful works of God—*** [publicly] [Ac.1:11] Those women certainly were not being *silent*.

The Road To Rediscovery

Jesus had lived with a passion to bring life, peace and happiness to hurting humanity. Now His followers, both men and women, had been impregnated with that same passion and had been endued with that same power. That was the driving force in their lives, and that power has not changed today.

Although it has taken centuries for Christian believers to rediscover the passion to witness about Christ, which was the secret of the soul-winning success of those First Century believers, that rediscovery has been made and is affecting the entire world today.

Multitudes of believers are taking their witness of Christ to needy people, out where they live and work and play. Jesus said, *My purpose is to invite sinners to turn from their sins, not to spend my time with those who think themselves already good enough.*^{Lu.5:32LB}

❖ ❖ ❖

IN OUR NEXT chapter I will share about my experience at a Methodist campmeeting and how I made the life-changing discovery that *Christ now expresses Himself through people like you and me.*

Do you know how *recently* the very first books or pamphlets were written on how to lead a person to Christ? You will see how rapidly this truth has spread throughout our world and why so many hundreds of thousands of people are receiving Christ as savior around the world.

Chapter 25

Witnesses Worldwide

THIS BOOK WAS first written during the early part of our world ministry. It consisted of *Seven Reasons Why We Are Soulwinners* (chapters 10 to 16 of this edition). It was one of the first books published to motivate Christian believers to witness and lead people to Christ *outside the church walls* — those who will not normally come into a sanctuary to hear the gospel.

We had committed our lives to ministry among what was then called *heathen* nations, sharing the gospel out on public fields or parks or in stadiums, proclaiming Christ to enormous multitudes of *non*-Christian people.

Multi-National Awakening

In every nation where we have conducted these great evangelism crusades and teaching seminars, there have been tremendous spiritual awakenings. Thousands of national believers have consecrated their lives to go throughout their own and other nations, as good news messengers for Christ. We have always urged them not to wait for some traditional *missionary call*, but to act on the words of Jesus and to go in His name, knowing that He has promised, *I am with you alway, even unto the end of the world.*Mt.28:20 He has said, *I will never leave you, nor forsake you.*He.13:5

Prior to each of our crusades, we always conduct a mass rally for Christians of the local churches, to inform them about *gospel ministry out on a public field* (which is very different than ministering to people inside the walls of a church sanctuary).

At these pivotal rallies, we teach thousands of believers concepts we present in this book. In nations where we have done this, there have been great outbreaks of soulwinning as national believers embrace these secrets that were so vital among First Century Christians.

Encouraging Believers

Throughout our decades of ministry, we have consistently taught that God makes no exception of persons, races, or sexes; that His call to every person who receives Christ, is to share His life and love with others.

We always emphasize the importance of the Holy Spirit in one's life to reflect Jesus. He said, *When the Comforter is come...he shall testify of me*.Jn.15:26 *He shall glorify* **me**: *for he shall receive of* **mine**, *and shall show it unto you*...Then He repeated: *he shall take of* **mine**, *and shall show it unto you*.Jn.16:14-15

In nation after nation, the results have been the same. Both men and women have gone out into the ripened harvest fields of their area, and of neighboring nations and have led many souls to Christ.

Worldwide Investment

Observing the results that these studies have had on national Christians around the world, we decided to publish them in a book which we called *Soulwining — Out Where The People Are.* Then we wrote a sequel which we entitled, *Outside The Sanctuary.* We mailed 125,000 gift copies of each of these books to leading missionaries and national preachers around the world.

These books were the seed-packets out of which has sprung the worldwide revival of *soulwinning outside the sanctuary.* Books focused on the subject of going out where the *unconverted* are and winning them there, had not been published at that time, so these two books made a worldwide impact on believers.

Torrey's Pacesetting Book

It may be a surprise to know that it was not until near the turn of the 20th century that Charles Spurgeon and R.A. Torrey wrote the first two little booklets about how a person could receive salvation. They dealt with how to help someone to receive Christ who had come to a public meeting, had answered an evangelist's call for salvation, and had come into the *inquirer's* room to be counseled.

Doing this was pace-setting and revolutionary, because Christians had been indoctrinated to believe that God's sovereign *Will* already determined who would be saved and who would be lost.

Divine Predestination
Or The Right To Choose

In the late 1800s, there was an *intense theological debate that raged among church leaders.* The issue was whether or not a person was predestined to be saved or lost, *or whether one could make a personal decision to accept Christ to be saved.* That seems ridiculous today, but from the 1500s, the doctrine of *Calvinism* insisted that the only persons who could come to God and receive salvation were those whom He had *predestined to be saved.*

The idea of convincing a person to *decide to accept Christ, on his or her own volition,* was considered by theologians to be heretical and humanistic. The concept was bitterly opposed.

Charles Finney Appears

Then the great preacher, Charles Finney, appeared on the scene. His preaching insisted that if a person heard the gospel, he or she had the innate prerogative of choice. One could make a personal decision to believe on Christ and be saved, or one had the right to reject the gospel.

He wrote his famous book, *Lectures on Revival.*

Finney was accused of being *carnal* in his ministry instead of *spiritual.* He was said to ignore God's sovereignty when he encouraged people to make a *rational* decision to be saved—as though human persons could be saved because they *wanted* to be. At that time, theologians considered the idea to be *un*biblical, even sacrilegious, an idea inspired by human logic and oblivious to the divine will of God.

But great evangelists like Finney, Spurgeon and Moody were bringing new light to the traditional Church. Paramount among their ideas was the developing wave of preaching, initiated by Wesley, Whitfield, Finney, and others, persuading sinners to make *rational, personal decisions* to accept Christ. They contended that God's gift of salvation *depended on one's personal engagement to believe on Christ, and not on some arbitrary doctrine of predestination.*

These evangelism leaders were bringing the Church to a new level of ministry, convincing people to accept Christ and to embrace Him as their savior and Lord — on *their own volition.* That was when R.A. Torrey wrote his classic, *How To Bring Men To Christ* (which should have been entitled How To Bring *People* To Christ, since they were persuading *women* as well as *men* to believe and be saved).

New Focus in Evangelism
Decisions in The Inquiry Room

Torrey was one of the most celebrated evangelists of the 19th century. His book, written and used almost exclusively in *Inquiry Rooms,* showed believers how to guide seekers of salvation to a *personal decision to accept Christ.* This instruction had not been published before, and it was pacesetting. But it did not address the idea of persuading *un*converted people *outside the meeting place.* That master key of First Century Christianity had not yet been rediscovered.

For seventy years after Torrey wrote his classic on how one can *personally decide for Christ,* practically every book or pamphlet on the subject that followed was a sort of re-write of his pacesetting script.

Hundreds of books and pamphlets on the subject have since been published. Practically every denomination has issued its version. *But they all came short of the passion of First Century Christians to go out where the people live and work and play, and win them **there***. It seems almost incredible that this teaching was delayed for such a long period.

Revelation At The Methodist Camp

In the 1960s, my older brother, Verl, a devoted Christian, took me to a Methodist campmeeting in eastern Oklahoma to hear the renowned Dr. Harry Denman who was the Secretary of the General Board of Evangelism of *The United Methodist Church* for 25 years. He was, without doubt, the greatest ambassador of *Love* I have ever met.

In that campmeeting, under Dr. Denman's inspired teaching, I received one of the great revelations of my life: *that the Christian believer is the living expression of Jesus today; that Jesus is alive in the believer; that the individual who accepts Him becomes His body in action today; that Jesus is made flesh in the person who receives Him.*

After that encounter, I wrote a sequel to *Soul-winning*, under the title, *Outside The Sanctuary*. Then we sent it abroad, as we had sent our previous book, to 125,000 missionaries and national preachers around the world.

Later, when we published a new edition of *Soulwinning,* we revised and enlarged it, including the text of *Outside The Sanctuary.* Today many ministers believe that this new edition of *"Soulwinning"* is the most important work I have authored.

Since these books were published and disseminated globally, hundreds of soulwinning societies and organizations have been raised up and are today winning millions of souls to Christ. They have published scores of dynamic books, pamphlets and audio and video courses that have brought a renewed soulwinning passion to the Church. As a result, multiplied millions of souls have been, and are being reached for Christ — *outside the walls of the sanctuary.*

Classic On Evangelism

It is hard to realize that this book, *Soulwinning,* has become such a *Classic On Evangelism.*

Some years ago, I addressed a convention of street preachers and founders of evangelism societies. I was overwhelmed to hear those leaders relate the inspiring influence that our soulwinning books had on them and how most of their lives had been transformed and most of their outside-the-church ministries had been birthed as a result.

Today the Church is experiencing the greatest worldwide sweep of soulwinning ever known. Evangelism leaders commonly target every residence in a nation and do not stop until each family has received a gospel witness.

Door To Door—Worldwide

One such association is currently reaching 350,000 homes for Christ each *week*, and their plan is to increase that number to 500,000. They have already distributed almost two *billion* tracts in 147 nations and each tract contains a response card. This has led to the formation of over 15,000 *Christ Groups* where no church existed before, and they project operations in every nation within a few years. This is reaching people for Christ out where they are. *This was the Master Key to the success of First Century Christians.*

Soulwinning triumphs like these are taking place around the world. In nations where the gospel is still forbidden or restrained today, national Christians are refusing to be intimidated by persecution and imprisonment. At great risk of their lives, they are distributing gospel portions and leading people to Christ as Early Church believers did.

It has been said that many former Soviet people "have Communist minds but Christian hearts." One evangelism society reports witnessing of Christ in seven million homes of four republics of the former Soviet Union, and they have already registered over a half-million responses to Christ. They say, "If we could find enough pastors, we could start new churches every day." No wonder Jesus said, *Pray therefore the Lord of the harvest, that he will send forth laborers into his harvest.*[Mt.9:39]

Out Where The People Are

Committed Christian believers around the world are recapturing the zeal and passion of Early Church believers. They are taking the witness of Jesus Christ out where the people are, and they are reaping the same harvests that Christians reaped in Bible days.

Jesus said, *The harvest truly is plenteous, but the laborers are few.*[Mt.9:37] Millions of people are waiting—outside the walls of the church building, out on the main roadways of life, where the rich and the poor, the beggar and the ruler travel together in search of truth. *There* is where they can be found and won to Christ. *There* is where Christ's followers, both men and women, are chosen and ordained by Him to *seek and to save those who are lost,*[Lu.19:10] **because *we are His witnesses.***[Ac.5:32]

✧ ✧ ✧

IN OUR NEXT chapter, we shall look at the remarkable significance of each individual's ministry, and the *gospel* that YOU are writing with your life.

Chapter 26

God's Connection

JESUS PREACHED SOME of His most significant sermons to *individuals* such as the noted Pharisee named Nicodemus,[Jn.3:1-8] or to the rich young ruler,[Lu.18:18-23] or to the Samaritan woman at the well,[Jn.4:6-30] etc.

Philip made a journey into the desert to witness of Christ to *one individual* — an Ethiopian eunuch,[Ac.8:26-29] and later, that African nation welcomed the gospel message.

Paul gave a most persuasive witness to Felix the governor, and almost persuaded him to become a Christian.[Ac.26:28]

When you begin to think of your own ministry of soulwinning, don't wait until you can witness to a crowd of people. Find someone who can be helped by knowing what Christ has done for you, and share your testimony. (Take advantage of the helpful and inspiring tools for soulwinners which are available from many reputable sources.)

One couple brought a hundred and twenty-nine new people into their church within two years because they went out witnessing as a regular part of their Christian lifestyle.

What might happen if church members systematically witnessed for Christ? When you begin to testify about experiences which you have had, other believers in your church will be inspired to follow your example. Soon, you may help motivate a fresh new revival in your church.

Every minute of every day, nearly a hundred souls slip into eternity. Before you go to church, before you pray at your church altar, before you go to bed, remember that nearly a hundred people *per minute* are dying and *most of them have never been exposed to the gospel.*

Ministry Of Excellence
Through Ordinary People

You cannot reach all who are *un*converted, but you can reach *some* of them. You are Christ's body—His feet, His arms, His lips, His voice. He can only reach lost souls through people like you. He has chosen to trust you with His message. You may regard others as more qualified than yourself but they are not. No one else can do *what you can do. YOU are unique—the only one of YOU that God has.*

Jesus chose average business and laboring people to be His witnesses. On the day of Pentecost, a hundred and twenty individuals were filled with the Holy Spirit and were empowered to be Christ's witnesses.^{Ac.1:8; 2:4} They were not professionals with degrees. They were common individual men and women who had met Jesus, who believed in His teachings and who had committed their lives to follow Him.

Persecution forced the early Christians to spread out from Jerusalem. *They that were scattered abroad went everywhere preaching the word.*^{Ac.8:4} Who was scattered? It was *the lay people,* **not** the apostles. *They were all scattered abroad...except the apostles.*^{Ac.8:1} Both the men and the women ^{Ac.8:3} *went everywhere preaching the word.*^{Ac.8:4}

The martyr, Stephen, and the evangelist, Philip, were common laypersons. The true Church is a people-movement—not an organization of ecclesiastics. It consists of individual believers in whom Christ is alive.

God has you where you are, to be His contact with people. The pastor may not be able to reach your contacts. You are there—among your classmates, in your factory, in your neighborhood. *You are God's connection with those around you.* You are His voice, His body. Be His witness. Let Him speak through you.

Writing Your Gospel

ANYONE WHO TRULY knows Christ, has something good to say about Him. Your Lord depends on you to express His love to *non-*Christians. *You are His Church in action today.*

Jesus Christ has done something good for you. You have a personal testimony. Share it with people. *When you tell what Christ has done for and through you, we could call your stories...*

The Gospel According To Y-O-U.

Matthew, Mark, Luke and John wrote their stories — their *gospels*. Paul spoke three times of his *gospel*.[Ro.2:16;16:25; 2Ti.2:8] Daisy and I have written ours. (It is entitled *The Gospel According to T.L. and Daisy*, — a 512 page classic documentary.)

Every day, *you* are recording *your gospel* by the words that you speak, by the stories that you relate of Christ's blessings, and by the deeds that you do as you *serve Him by serving people.*

✧ ✧ ✧

HERE IN BRIEF, is the case for Christian soul-winning in a nutshell:

1. YOUR *CALLING*: Every Believer A Witness.

Christian means Christlike. Christ was the greatest soulwinner. *He came to seek and to save the lost.*[Lu.19:10] He told His first followers to be *fishers of people.*[Mk.1:17] He told His last followers to communicate the gospel to *every creature.*[Mk.16:15]

To be *Christlike* (a Christian) is to be a *soulwinner* — to be Christ inhabited, to be Christ's body in action today.

2. YOUR *FIELD*: Out Where The People Are.

Reach the *un*churched, the down-and-outers, the *non*-Christians. They will listen. They need you. The *un*converted do not go to church. Christ can never reach most of them there in the sanctuary. They can only be reached through people like you and like me, who will go witness to them *out where they are.*

You can find them on street corners, in private homes, in stores, in slums, at bedsides, in marketplaces, at beaches, in jails, in prisons or other detention centers, in hospitals, in resort areas, at fairs, in clubs, in parks, at zoos, at entertainment centers — wherever people are.

They are there by the millions — the *un*converted, the *un*churched — those who are lonely, *un*loved, ignored, frightened, insecure, angry, demoralized, abusive, offensive, despairing, guilty, weary, confused.

There they wait for a kind voice and a simple gesture of compassion. They are desperate, suspicious, sick, incurable, homeless, loveless, suffering, disheartened, depressed, ashamed, friendless, abused, grief-stricken, miserable, exploited, lost, without hope and without God, existing, waiting and dying—little by little, in a darkened world, alone. And that is the darkness where Christ's light in your life can shine the brightest.

Lead them to Christ. Let Him speak to them through your lips. They will respond to your witness of hope and of love and will soon become witnesses of Christ to their own acquaintances.

3. YOUR *GOAL*: Adding Souls To The Church.

It is not enough to witness or to win souls. They should be influenced into a church where a faithful pastor can help them to grow in bible faith and in God's grace.

Stamp the literature you distribute with your church address. Welcome new contacts to your congregation. Meet them there. Introduce them to Christians—and to your pastor.

Then visit them. See that they receive good literature. Inform them about church meetings and help them to become acquainted with other believers so they will feel comfortable. And remember that you can continue to influence them in their spiritual growth, so maintain sensitive contact with them.

◇ ◇ ◇

IN 1950, we conducted a five-week evangelistic and healing crusade at the beautiful 5,000 seat Masonic Temple in Detroit, Michigan. We ministered as a team with the senior evangelist F.F. Bosworth, a renowned contemporary of the celebrated Evangelist Aimee Semple McPherson.

This valiant servant of God often quoted, what Jesus said: *You shall know the truth, and the truth shall make you free.*[Jn.8:32] Rev. Bosworth would say: "It's the *truth* that blesses people. Whether it comes through an *oral voice or through the printed page, its power is the same."*

That is what our next chapter is about.

Chapter 27

Where No Voice Speaks

EVERY CHRISTIAN who wants to win souls to Christ should discover the power of the printed page. There is a renowned saying, *"The pen is mightier than the sword."*

The written word can penetrate where the human voice is forbidden. It needs no passport and has no visa problems. It travels economically, leaps language barriers and is never influenced by racial, sexual or social prejudices.

The written word can sail the oceans, trek the deserts, and trudge the jungle footpaths of every continent on earth. It can penetrate the crowded cities and reach the sparsely settled countryside, entering sophisticated mansions and village cottages alike.

The written word can tell its story in homes or shops, in factories or in fields. It can penetrate the forgotten areas where people are too poor or too primitive to have access to radio or television. In

357

areas where the reception of electronic signals is practically nil due to mountain ranges or other interference, the persistent and practical ministry of printed preachers is never thwarted.

The written word is often more powerful than the human voice. They said of Paul, *His letters are weighty and powerful, but his bodily presence is weak, and his speech contemptible.*2Co.10:10

Unrelenting Messenger

The written word knows no fear and flinches in the face of no opponent. It preaches the same message to the rich and to the poor, to the king and to the commoner. It never loses its temper nor retaliates in anger. It is oblivious to scoffs, jeers, or insults.

The printed word never tires, but witnesses twenty-four hours a day wherever people want to learn. It is never discouraged, but will tell its story over and over again. It will speak to a single individual as willingly as to a multitude. It always catches a person in the right mood to be receptive, for it only speaks when someone chooses to listen.

The printed word can be received, read, and studied in private or in secret, amidst tumult or in tranquillity. And it speaks without a foreign accent.

The written word never compromises or changes its message. It continues to speak long after audible words have been forgotten and their sound has dissipated.

The written word continues to witness and to influence people long after its author has died. The works of Luther, Calvin, and Knox are still being circulated more than four hundred years after their demise. And think of the Bible itself. What a graphic illustration of the power and permanence of the printed page!

The Wonder Of Witnessing

Would you like to win souls? If you are a committed Christian, no doubt your answer is a resounding "Yes." You can win souls.

Only a small percentage of Christians can be full-time workers, evangelists, pastors, missionaries, teachers, or writers; but *every believer* can win people through the printed page.

Peter Cartwright, the famous circuit rider and pioneer evangelist, said, "For more than fifty years I have firmly believed that it is part and parcel of a Christian's sacred duty to circulate religious literature. The religious press is destined, under the order of providence, to minister salvation's grace to the perishing millions of the earth."

We have shared that attitude for over a half century. *A veritable river of literature has poured from our offices to all corners of the earth in a hundred and thirty-two major languages and dialects*

Having studied the methods used by atheistic propagandists to dominate public opinion, one renowned authority says: "It is urgent that we saturate nations with *Christian* literature. I know of no other project so urgently needed or that will pay such rich dividends in winning souls."

In more than eighty countries, I have seldom seen a person toss aside a gospel tract. But I have often witnessed them fighting over printed messengers of Christ when there were not enough copies available for everyone.

Millions of hands are reaching out to us for these printed portions of the Bread of Life — these *printed preachers*. It is the Christian's greatest opportunity to help fill those hands with the truth of the gospel, around the world

May God grant that you too will become a good news messenger to needy people through the power of the printed page and through many other *Soulwinning Tools* that are available today from various reputable Christian institutions.*

---

* Request a free brochure that lists all *T.L., Daisy and LaDonna Osborn* books, audio and video cassettes, docu-miracle films, Bible study courses, tracts or other publications and productions. Address: **OSFO Int'l, Box 10, Tulsa, OK 74102 USA**

✧ ✧ ✧

NOW WE WILL share some practical ideas that can serve as effective guidelines for you in witnessing to people and leading them to Christ.

Chapter 28

Ideas For Sharing Christ

HERE ARE SOME ideas to help Christian believers to effectively witness for Christ. The laity often holds the opinion that soulwinning is a complex art. It is not. *It is one person talking to another person about Jesus Christ and what He means in their life — here and now.*

The *un*converted world is not very interested in what a *preacher behind some pulpit* has to say about spiritual things. But every human being wants to know about God or Jesus or the Bible or faith or miracles or prayer, *if they can hear it from some non-ecclesiastical person whom they trust.*

I have observed that almost any committed Christian believer loves to tell others what God has done in his or her life, when they can talk about Him in normal conversation. Millions of *un*believers are curious about what Christians experience in their rapport with Christ. They will listen to such *witnesses.*

Openers For Witnessing

HERE ARE SOME ideas for dialogue with an *unsaved* person about Christ.

Sometimes concepts about witnessing make a believer feel that he or she should be able to answer any question on any subject with *thus saith the Lord*. And this can be intimidating to the soulwinner.

How many times have you wanted to witness to someone but you could not manage to steer the conversation. Rather than to appear to be awkward, you let the opportunity pass.

Here are some simple "approach sentences" which you may find useful. This first one is an ideal "opener."

✧ ✧ ✧

1st: *"Have you ever given much thought to spiritual matters?"*

Make the question natural and thoughtful.

Its purpose is to center the thoughts of the *unconverted* person on spiritual values — without being too abrupt or direct.

You may word the question in any way that will make it flow more smoothly for you. For example, you might say:

"We came to visit you because we'd like to get better acquainted. Mary and I have made a lot of wonderful friends this way. We've been Christians for several years and we've been so happy. I don't know what your attitude is about God, but He has made a great difference in our lives. By the way, *have you ever given much thought to spiritual things?*"

Or you might be discussing your favorite hobbies and say: "I'm glad to know about your interests. I guess that's how we get better acquainted. John and I are Christians and we really have a happy life. *Have you and your spouse ever thought much about spiritual things?*"

POSSIBLE REPLY: "Oh, I guess we have. Not as much as we ought to, though."

You can expect a rather general response. Some people may take ten minutes to answer; others, only a brief yes or no. Avoid interrupting their reply. Let them talk. Listen. Learn how they think. Your questions are only to get them to open up. Your time to talk is after the door is open. If you are a good listener, you earn the right to be heard by them when you talk.

IMPORTANT: Whatever their reply to your first "approach," move to the next question.

❖ ❖ ❖

2nd: *"What would you say is a human person's greatest spiritual need?"*

Remember you are the inquirer, not the teacher. Listen to their reply. They may tell you about some problem or some philosophy about life. Listen to them talk because you will learn about them and will be able to share your witness of Christ in a way that is not offensive to them. It is very important that they feel that you are someone who understands.

The one you are speaking to will begin to have confidence that he or she can discuss this subject without pressure from you, and may even bring up their own need of salvation. If they do, your "approach" has already opened the door.

You may reword this second question to fit the conversation better, such as: "People are talking so much about physical needs today, but spiritual needs are important too. *What would you say is a human person's greatest spiritual need?"*

POSSIBLE REPLY: "Oh, I don't know; being good, or believing in God, I suppose."

You'll hear many replies. Remember not to interrupt. It will give you a good idea of the person's attitude. No matter what their answer is, move to your next question.

❖ ❖ ❖

3rd: *"You know, God tells us that a human person's greatest spiritual need is a real experience of salvation. Have you ever thought about your own need of salvation?"*

You have not assumed that he or she is, or is not saved. Their answer should let you know. It will cause that person to think about any serious religious experience or maybe death, etc. It will indicate his or her personal religious condition. If the person is saved, your question will still be taken well.

POSSIBLE REPLY: "Oh, sure, just about everyone has thought about that at some time." Almost always that third question will cause them to relate some incident. If they talk, listen. Then go on to your fourth question.

✧ ✧ ✧

4th: *"What would you say a person needs to do to be saved?"*

This is a most vital question. Their reply will let you know what they understand of the gospel. They will likely enjoy answering this question. Most *non*-Christians will come up with one of the "do-it-yourself" answers:

POSSIBLE REPLY: "Always do your best. Pay your bills. Be kind to animals." Or "Go to church; be baptized, and pray."

They may even apply the matter personally and protest, "Oh, I never do anybody any harm. I'll be all right."

With that fourth question, you are finding out if your subject is saved or not. If you asked directly, "Are you saved?" or "Are you a Christian?", they might tell you that they are. Then you could not question their experience without risking an argument.

If a conflict evolves in your discussion, then you might win the argument but you will probably lose the chance to guide a soul to Christ. So do your best to avoid disputes. Stay on ground where you can appear agreeable, but keep steering the conversation your way.

EXCEPTION: If the person answers your fourth question with an honest..."Well, I don't know" or "I couldn't say," then skip the fifth question and, instead, show them God's word.

But usually your fourth question will draw them out. Most people have a definite, though perhaps a strange opinion about getting salvation. They generally believe in doing good works of some kind. When he or she gives you their opinion, listen to it. It is vital that you know what they think. Then you can go on to your fifth question.

✧ ✧ ✧

5th: *"Yes, you're right, everyone ought to do those things. But what I really meant was: How to go about receiving salvation?"*

POSSIBLE REPLY: Whatever the reply, appear to agree with them that their idea is good — and it usually will have merit, but then go on to your sixth question.

✧ ✧ ✧

6th: *"Yes, and you know, it's really even simpler than that. Could I show you three or four verses* (casually pull out your New Testament) *of what the Bible says about salvation?"*

POSSIBLE REPLY: The person you are witnessing to will usually say, "Sure, go ahead," or "Of course, I don't mind."

NOTE: Someone might say, "Oh, I've read the Bible." Simply respond, "Oh, I'm sure you have — and I'll bet you've found it interesting too. Notice here, these verses." They'll look with you.

✧ ✧ ✧

Witness And Decision

NOW THE DOOR is open for your simple five-point witness. Don't preach. Use no more than a few verses in the Bible. Make your points clear and remember that your goal is a decision for Christ.

I suggest these verses and this outline:

1. *People's need* — *Romans 3:23*

2. *Sin's penalty* — *Romans 6:23a*

3. *Christ's remedy* — *Romans 5:8*

4. *God's gift to people* — *Romans 6:23b*

5. *How to receive* — *Romans 10:9,10,13.*

You can mark these verses in the margin of your New Testament as a chain of references to follow. Notice that all of them are in the book of Romans, quite near each other, so you can casually refer to them.

Remember to be brief and do not ask questions. State facts and assume that your potential convert agrees with what you say.

Be positive and give the impression that you believe he or she is glad about the facts which you are sharing about salvation.

Conclude promptly by suggesting: "John (or Mary) — (call them by name), these are wonderful truths. I know you appreciate how easy God has made it for anyone to be saved. He says to confess your sin and to ask Him to forgive you. When you do this, He comes into your life and saves you!"

✧ ✧ ✧

THEN SAY, quietly:

"If you don't mind, I'd like to have a brief word of prayer with you."

Don't wait for the person's permission. Bow your head and close your eyes — and keep talking:

"While I pray, just close your eyes and bow your head with me. The Lord is right here with us now. He loves you and wants to bless you and your home more than ever before."

✧ ✧ ✧

NOW PRAY:

Lord Jesus, thank You for making it possible for us to be saved. Help John (or Mary — call their names) to see that You are here to save them right now. Help them to call upon the name of the Lord Jesus. Save John (Mary) right now, Lord. Let the real joy of forgiveness and peace come to them at this moment.

If your friend is a parent, pray for God to show him or her that their children need a Christian home. But be brief. Make it short and to the point.

✧ ✧ ✧

IMPORTANT: Do not close your prayer with, "In Jesus' name, Amen!" If you do, the person will look up and your opportunity to get their decision may be lost.

Instead of closing your prayer, with your head still bowed in a position of prayer, simply begin talking to your friend again.

Say, "John (Mary), while our heads are bowed and our eyes are closed, ask the Lord Jesus to save you right now. Just say:

DEAR LORD, I want to receive you in my life."

Wait for him or her to repeat it. *This is the moment you have waited for.* You have done all you can do. Christ is there. Your friend must now say *Yes* or *No* – to Him. If he or she is being drawn by Christ's Spirit and has decided to follow Him, they will repeat the prayer.

Sometimes, they may continue the prayer without further prompting. If so, join them in your heart. Or they may repeat your first line, then wait. Then continue guiding them in prayer, line by line, and do it with confidence that this is the moment when God's Spirit is at work.

CONTINUE THE PRAYER:

I call upon Your name.

Forgive all of my sins.

I believe You died in my place.

I accept You as my personal savior.

I believe You rose from the dead according to the scriptures.

I receive You into my life.

I believe You do save me now.

Thank You, Jesus, for my salvation. Amen!

◇ ◇ ◇

AFTER YOUR CONTACT has accepted Christ, you can help him or her in many ways.

They will now have confidence in you and will feel that they can trust you. They know that you care about them. They will likely be glad to accompany you to your church because they are grateful that you have shared Christ with them. Keep in close contact with them and get them acquainted with other believers.

Arrange to take them to church, or set a time and be at the door when they arrive. Introduce them to Christian friends and fellow church members. At your earliest opportunity, introduce them to your pastor. Tell the pastor about their conversion.

Encourage them to read the Bible daily.

Visit them at intervals. When possible, read the Bible with them. Welcome them into a Bible class. This person is now brother or sister in Christ. Before long, he or she will be going with you, visiting other people, learning how to witness, and soon you will have produced another soulwinner in your church.

◇ ◇ ◇

HERE ARE THE suggested questions to open a soulwinning conversation:

1. Have you ever given much thought to spiritual matters?

2. What would you say is a human person's greatest spiritual need?

3. Have you ever thought about your own need of salvation?

4. What would you say a person needs to do to be saved?

5. How do you go about receiving salvation?

6. Could I show you three or four verses about what the Bible says a person must do to receive salvation?

The Bible says: *They that be wise shall shine as the brightness of the firmament; and they that turn many to righteousness as the stars for ever and ever.*[Da.12:3]

Chapter 29

Concepts For Soulwinners

THERE IS NO PURPOSE in fighting problems. Those who succeed in soulwinning are people who create solutions.

Ministering in some eighty different nations of the world, we have had to be solution people. One of the ideas God planted in our hearts, one that has resulted in millions of souls being saved, is the use of *Tools for Evangelism*. In an epoch of electronic technology, of high speed presses and of space-age magnetic reproduction, *there are so many ways to multiply and to compound our witness of Christ to people.*

The Printed Preacher

WE WROTE EIGHTEEN tracts that build faith for the blessings provided in Christ's salvation. We wrote them in vocabulary that is so basic that a child can grasp their simple gospel messages.

These have been translated and published in *one hundred thirty-two languages*. For years they have poured from gospel presses at the rate of a ton per day. National church leaders, missionaries, gospel workers and Christians around the world use them and acclaim them as among the very best that they have used.

We provide sets of negatives, in whatever languages we possess, for pastors and national leaders who defray the costs of reproducing, handling and shipping them. We grant permission for them to be published locally by national churches or Christian societies.

Marxists made their greatest advances in the world through the influence of the printed page. They considered communist literature to be more effective than their tanks and bombs. The Bible and good Christian literature are the most effective tools that believers can use.

A friendly smile, an offered tract and a word of testimony can open the door to a soulwinning encounter that can lead to another conversion.

The Magnetic Message

IN MANY NATIONS, a large percent of believers find it difficult to share the gospel because they lack knowledge of the Bible.

To facilitate believers in witnessing, we have recorded gospel messages that have proved effective around the world. They have been interpreted, phrase by phrase, on audio tape, by good national interpreters, in nearly seventy major languages and dialects.

We provide master copies of these messages for pastors and Christian leaders (for the costs of production, handling and shipping), along with authorization to duplicate them in any quantity, for witnessing or for sale. Christian believers can carry these messages and proclaim the good news in homes, villages, towns, hospitals, office and apartment complexes, market places and wherever *un*converted people can be reached.

More souls are being won to Christ through our audio tapes than through our own personal ministry of mass evangelism.

Christian workers who play these cassettes for the *un*saved, are simultaneously getting a practical exposure to effective gospel ministry. After the Christian worker has heard these messages a few times, they begin to preach them too—as effectively as anyone can.

If Paul Had A Recorder

Think of Paul, dictating his weighty letters to a scribe who had no typewriter, carbon paper, ballpoint pen or even a lead pencil. What might he have accomplished with a good audio cassette recorder? He would have doubtless duplicated every message possible and sent it by runners to the ends of his world. That is what we are doing as another soulwinning outreach of this world ministry.

Even believers who are not preachers, when equipped with audio cassette players, can witness successfully and win souls to Christ. Jesus said, *the truth will make you free.*[Jn.8:32] Whether preached or printed or recorded, wherever truth is received, its power is the same.

With gospel audio cassettes, believers can evangelize in their own residence or in the homes of friends, in jails, hospitals, and at the bedsides of invalids. (An ear attachment can avoid disturbing others.)

Amplification can help share each message with groups, in homes for the elderly, in market places, or anywhere else that people can listen.

Reaching Lonely People

There are exciting possibilities during vacation seasons. People have periods of leisure at seasides or mountain resorts, on country ranches or at entertainment centers, at home or abroad. Thousands spend empty hours in boredom. They offer ideal opportunities for your audio cassette and tract ministries.

Organize teams of fellow Christians to go with you. With modern *Soulwinning Tools*, any believer can amplify his or her ministry and effectively win more people to Christ.

A seventy-three year-old woman bought an audio cassette player so that she and her seventy-six year old sister could visit hospitals, the local jail, homes for senior citizens and shut-ins, and other areas with their gospel witness.

In her letter to us, she said, "We are old on the outside, but we are young on the inside. Though we are advanced in years, with these *tools,* we are able to share Christ with others."

Churches can maintain a library of audio and video cassettes, and lend them to Christians who have a passion for souls. The laity can utilize these *tools* to help many people discover new life in Jesus Christ.

Faith Building Faith Library

BOOKS THAT BLESS and inspire people are priceless treasures. We have written and published many powerful and positive books about faith, salvation, healing and soulwinning. They are written for all believers, regardless of social status, race, color or gender. *Daisy's five major books, written to encourage women in God's work, are unprecedented in Christian literature for women.*

Our practical, positive books constitute a faith-building tool chest to help believers win more souls. They are packed with much that is valuable to soulwinners and is challenging for new converts. Churches and Christians can establish lending libraries, circulating them among converts and acquaintances. They also make valued gifts to share with others.

The *un*beatable Tool

NO TOOL, ancient or modern, has surpassed the effectiveness of our *Docu-Miracle Films* (or videos) as dynamic soul-harvesters, both at home and abroad.

A French philosopher said: "The public no longer looks to the Church for truth—they look to the world of film productions and of television." He meant that the Church has become so ritualistic that it no longer attracts the attention of the new generation.

Youth absorbs their life philosophies of life through the medium of cinematography. The result is too often perversion and confusion in society—not because motion photography is evil, but because of the demoralizing violence, brutality and social promiscuity that is so often portrayed.

Our Re-Beginning

In 1947 the Lord Jesus appeared to me. I became convinced that the same miracles wrought in Bible days are for today; that only miracles would convince humanity that Jesus Christ is alive and *un*changed today. Daisy and I realized that in many lands, dead gods, idols, fetishes and graven images are worshipped because people do not know the living God. So we set out to proclaim the gospel in *non*-Christian nations.

Like the apostle Paul, *We strived to preach the gospel, not where Christ was named, lest [we] should build upon another's foundation.*[Ro.15:20]

We were persuaded that if the people could witness the power of God to heal the sick, as it was manifested in Bible days, they would accept Jesus Christ and become His followers.

We have gone from nation to nation, conducting gospel crusades out in public places so that all people of all faiths can feel welcome. We proclaim the gospel then we urge each person to make a decision for Christ. After that, we pray for the sick. Each miracle is proof that Christ is the living savior and that His promises are true.

Tens of thousands of *non*-Christian people have been convinced of the gospel and have made public decisions to embrace Christ. Multitudes are added to the churches wherever our crusades are conducted. The results are invariably the same regardless of national heritage, religion or cultural background.

Docu-Miracle Film Concept

Our docu-miracle film ministry was conceived to capture the messages and miracles of some of our historic evangelism crusades. Today thousands of those films and videos are circulated internationally, in about seventy major languages. Gospel workers in scores of nations use them, attracting large crowds of people to hear of Christ.

Those films and videos have proven to be among the most effective *Tools For Evangelism* yet produced for reaching the *un*reached, for national church growth, and for home-front witnessing among the *un*converted.

Cinematography For God

In emerging nations, large business companies utilize motion films and videos to propagate and to market their secular products among millions of people, realizing handsome financial profits.

The Marxists exploited cinematography as one of their most forceful influences. Film technology may be among the most dynamic tools known, to persuade human society. Hollywood has demonstrated its effectiveness for both good and for evil.

Rather than to lament the demoralizing use of a potentially good technology, the prerogative of the Christian Church is to *exploit this science for propagating the gospel* of the living Christ.

Productions like ours that combined **missionary preaching** with **miracles** among *non*-Christian nations *had not existed before ours were produced*. Public mass evangelism meetings in *non*-Christian lands, accompanied by signs, miracles and wonders, *had not yet occurred in the age of cinematography*.

The First Mass Miracle Crusades Since The First Century Church

We were the *first* to install a big platform, lights and public address system out on parks or fields or terrains, in *non*-Christian nations, and to preach the gospel publicly, praying for God's miraculous confirmation that Jesus Christ is the same today as He was in Bible days.

Those visual tools created by recording those apostolic crusades and biblical wonders — *live,* are not for church entertainment. They are a dynamic attraction for *un*converted people to hear the gospel and to see it confirmed by miracles.

Showing The Way

During vacations, at the beach, in the mountains, or on any campground, many will come and view a film just to pass the time. Once people witness Christ's power, they will stay and listen to you talk because they will want to know Christ in a personal way.

These docu-miracle films are available (for their production, handling and mailing costs), in various major languages, on videos—¾" U-Matic or ½" VHS in the NTSC, PAL or SECAM formats.

BEYOND THE CHURCH WALLS

Educational Institutions

IN CONTEMPLATING your field of evangelism, remember that these docu-miracle films are effective ministry tools to use in schools, colleges, universities, summer camps, vacation centers, nurses training schools, orphanages, institutes of correction, etc. They will normally be admitted on an *educational* basis. You will usually be given liberty to speak before or after your film showing.

Public Institutions

Hospitals, homes for the aged, sanitariums, institutions for the handicapped, shelters, prisons, juvenile detention centers, and scores of other places are wonderful environments for evangelism. *Remember that even **deaf** people can watch a film. **Blind** people can listen to a gospel audio cassette.*

There is a tremendous field of opportunity in the penal institutions, reformatories and correctional institutions.

And how about homes for unwed mothers, alcoholic and narcotic rehabilitation institutes, government projects, military bases and special housing projects.

Reaching Out To People

Have you thought about refugee camps? Wherever there are groups of people of other nationalities, they constitute a ripe and responsive field for evangelism when you have *Soulwinning Tools* in these languages.

These docu-miracle films, audio and video cassettes, tracts and books are available (at the costs of producing, handling and mailing), in almost seventy major languages like Spanish, Urdu, Hindi, Tamil, Mandarin, Cantonese, Tagalog, Cebuano, Ilongo, French, Italian, German, or others.

You may have received a missionary call but were never able to go abroad yourself. This is a way you can become a missionary on your own home front and perhaps win more souls than if you had gone to another nation.

Ministering Love
In A Hurting World

Think of amusement areas, fairs and expositions; lodges, factories, clubs, bars, and taverns; apartment buildings, street corners, parks, plazas, market places; beaches, mountain resorts, health spas, vacation villages or camps. Wherever there are people, souls can be won.

These tools can open the doors in wealthy residential homes as well as in slums and ghettos. Rescue missions, Salvation Army hostels and flophouses are also potential areas.

You can show films or videos, and share books and tracts at missionary rallies, youth crusades, youth meetings and events; in public halls or wherever people congregate.

With a docu-miracle film festival as the center of your witness, your church can reach new districts for Christ in house to house soulwinning. An invitation to a docu-miracle film service in a neutral place can attract people who would never attend a church meeting.

The good news of Christ's salvation is the only hope for millions who exist in hopeless despair all over the world. For every soul won to Christ, nearly fifty more people are born into *non-*Christian homes.

Technology For Witnessing

The business world exploits each new technology to promote its secular products in every possible public market of today's world. Popular or practical products are available internationally, even in the most remote areas — in many regions where the gospel has not yet penetrated.

Marxists did not fail to seize available techniques of propaganda. With them they influenced entire nations. Films, records, tapes, videos and the printed page proved to be of greater value to them than bombs, tanks and guns. Their ideology penetrated thousands of villages and subverted whole nations. How is it that they reached so many so soon, when the Church has not reached them for so long?

These soulwinning tools are productive talents for Christian laypersons, for evangelists, for pastors, for Bible Schools and for churches.

Jesus gave an example of a man in Matthew 25:14-30, who delivered his goods into the hands of his servants, expecting that they would increase them while he was on a journey. It was a story to inspire us to put the talents to work that He has entrusted us with, so that, at His return, His Kingdom would be increased.

According to His parable, the Lord will say: *Well done, you good and faithful servant. For unto* *everyone that **has** shall be given, and he or she shall have abundance.* Clearly our Lord wants us to win souls, to increase His family of believers.

◇ ◇ ◇

IN THE FINAL chapter of this book, we offer the reader five facts about being saved, seven steps to receive Jesus Christ as Lord, a prayer to confess faith in Him, and a place to register the decision of whoever takes this action.

If you have not made a personal commitment of your life to Christ as your Lord and savior, resolve to do so while reading this final chapter.

If you are already a Christian believer, we offer these fundamentals as guidelines to assist you in leading others to salvation.

Chapter 30

The Biblical Christian

YOU MAY NOT be sure that you have been born again. Or you may have subscribed to a religion or joined a church without experiencing the miracle of the new birth. If that should be your case, the Bible says that you can *know* [you can be certain] *that you have passed from death unto life.*[1Jn.3:14]

This chapter will help you to experience this miracle. It can take place in you while you read this with reverence and simple faith.

If you are already a Christian, this chapter can guide you in showing others how to experience the miracle of salvation.

The Bible says, *This is a faithful saying, and worthy of all acceptation, that Christ Jesus came into the world to save sinners.*[1Ti.1:15]

It says, *God sent not His Son into the world to condemn the world; but that the world through Him might be saved.*[1Jn.3:17]

Peter said, *Whoever shall call on the name of the Lord shall be saved.*[Ac.2:21]

What does it mean to be *saved*?

✧ ✧ ✧

FIRST

To be saved means:
To be born again, to become a child of God.

Jesus said, *You must be born again.*[Jn.3:7] Christ actually enters your life and you are made new because He begins to live in you. This is not accepting a religion. This is accepting Christ. He is a person, not a philosophy. He is reality, not theory.

When I was married and accepted Daisy as my wife. I did not get the marriage religion. I received a person—Daisy, who became my wife, and my life was changed as a result.

When I was saved by receiving Christ, I did not accept the Christian religion. I received a Person—the Lord Jesus, as my savior, and my life was transformed accordingly.

My conversion was as definite as my marriage was. On both occasions, I received another person into my life.

The Bible says, *As many as received Him, to them He gave the power to become the children of God.*[Jn.1:12]

What a marvel that a human person can receive a new birth and be born into God's royal family!

You have been born once—a natural birth, of human parents who were descendants of Adam and Eve and whose sin against God was transmitted to all of the human race. It was their sin that estranged you and me from God. Now Christ says, *You must be born again.*[Jn.3:7] He invites you to become a friend of God, to be converted, saved, changed, recreated, to experience a new kind of *Life* — His *Life*.

◇ ◇ ◇

SECOND

To be saved means:
To have your sins forgiven.

The Psalmist David said, *He forgives all your iniquities.*[Ps.103:3]

The angel said, *You shall call His name Jesus: for he shall save His people from their sins.*[Mt.1:21]

God says, *I am He who blots out your transgressions.*[Is.43:25] *Their sins and iniquities will I remember no more.*[He.10:17] *As far as the east is from the west, so far has He removed our transgressions from us.*[Ps.103:12]

◇ ◇ ◇

THIRD

To be saved means:
To receive a new spiritual life.

Paul says, *If any one be in Christ, that person is a new creature: old things are passed away; behold all things are become new.*[2Co.5:17]

That is exactly what happens when Jesus Christ saves you. A creative miracle takes place. Old desires, habits, and diseases pass away. Everything becomes new. You receive a new life, a new nature, new health, new desires, new ambitions. You receive Christ's *Life.*

He said, *I am come that you might have life, and that you might have it more abundantly.*[Jn.10:10]

◇ ◇ ◇

FOURTH

To be saved means:
To receive peace.

Jesus said, *Peace I leave with you. My peace I give unto you.*[Jn.14:27] He said, *I have spoken unto you, that in me you might have peace.*[Jn.16:33]

Real peace only comes with Christ's pardon and His gift of salvation. Living in sin you can never have peace in your soul. The Bible says, *There is no peace, says my God, to the wicked.*[Is.57:21]

But *being justified by faith, we have peace with God through our Lord Jesus Christ.*[Ro.5:1]

✧ ✧ ✧

FIFTH

To be saved means:
To have fellowship with God.

You were created in God's likeness, so that you could walk and talk with Him. But your sins separated you from God. Now, instead of fellowship with the Father, you fear God. The thought of facing Him frightens you. Your sins condemn you and they create in you a sense of guilt and insecurity before Him.

Only Christ can save you from your sins. He will blot out every stain and bring you back to God with a clean record—as if you had never sinned. Then you can say with John in the New Testament: *Truly our fellowship is with the Father, and with His Son Jesus Christ.*[1Jn.1:3] God will be *a friend that sticks closer than a brother or a sister.*[Pr.18:24]

How To *Know* You Are Saved

No PERSON WAS made for a life of sin and disease. People were created to walk with God. But sin has separated humanity from Him.

Your iniquities have separated between you and your God, and your sins have hid His face from you,

393

that He will not hear.[Is.59:2] But, His blood was shed for many, *for the remission of sins.*[Mt.26:28]

John said, *If we confess our sins* [to Him], *He is faithful and just to forgive us our sins, and to cleanse us from all unrighteousness.*[1Jn.1:9] Then he added, *We know that we have passed from death unto life.*[1Jn.3:14]

There are many things in this world which we may never know, but we can *know* that we have Christ's life in us. We can know that we have been saved — that we are born again.

To say, "I don't know for sure if I'm saved," is like a husband or a wife saying, "I don't know for sure if I'm married."

To say, "I think I'm saved; I try to be, but I'm not sure about it," is like saying, "I think I'm married; I try to be, but I'm not sure about it."

Jesus said, *Anyone who believes* [the gospel] *and is baptized shall be saved.*[Mk.16:16]

Paul said, *If you shall confess with your mouth the Lord Jesus, and shall believe in your heart that God has raised Him from the dead, you shall be saved.*[Ro.10:9]

These scriptures promise: *You shall be saved.* Do what they say, and you can know that you have received Christ — that you have passed from death unto life, that you are saved. This is not accepting a religion. This is receiving Christ.

A real Christian is a person who...

1. Has come to God to be forgiven of sin and to receive a new life from Him;

2. Has accepted the Lord Jesus Christ as his or her personal savior by embracing Him as Lord and Master;

3. Has confessed Christ as Lord before others.

4. Is striving to please Him every day.

Seven Steps To Salvation

IF YOU ARE not sure that you have personally accepted Jesus Christ into your heart as your Lord and Master, then follow these seven steps prayerfully and you will receive a miraculous spiritual experience in which He will come to you and will begin living in and through you.

FIRST: Realize that you have sinned.

Paul said that *All have sinned, and have come short of the glory of God.*[Ro.3:23]

John added, *If we say that we have no sin, we deceive ourselves.*[1Jn.1:8]

SECOND: Truly repent of your sins.

Jesus illustrated this attitude: *And the publican, standing afar off, would not lift up so much as his eyes* unto heaven, but smote upon his breast, saying, God be merciful to me a sinner.[Lu.18:13]

Paul said, For godly sorrow works repentance to salvation.[2Co.7:10]

THIRD: Confess your sins to God.

The Bible says, One who covers sin shall not prosper: but whoever confesses and forsakes them shall have mercy.[Pr.28:13]

John said, If we confess our sins [to Him], He is faithful and just to forgive us our sins, and to cleanse us from all unrighteousness.[1Jn.1:9]

FOURTH: Forsake your sins.

Isaiah, the prophet said, Let the wicked forsake their way, and the unrighteous their thoughts; and let them return to the Lord, and He will have mercy upon them…for He will abundantly pardon.[Is.55:7]

Solomon said, Whoever confesses and forsakes sin shall have mercy.[Pr.28:13]

FIFTH: Ask forgiveness for your sins.

David the Psalmist said that God is the One Who forgives all your iniquities.[Ps.103:3]

Isaiah the prophet said, Come now, and let us reason together, says the Lord: though your sins be as scarlet, *they shall be white as snow; though they be red like crimson, they shall be as wool.*Is.1:18

SIXTH: Consecrate your entire life to Christ.

Jesus said, *Whoever shall confess me before others, I will confess that one before my Father which is in heaven.*Mt.10:32

*But you are a chosen generation...that you should show forth the praises of Him who has called you out of darkness into His marvelous light.*1Pe.2:9

SEVENTH: Believe that God saves you by His grace.

Paul said, *For by grace are you saved through faith; and that not of yourselves; it is the gift of God: not of works, lest any one should boast.*Ep.2:8-9

Accept Christ Now

*NOW IS THE accepted time; behold, now is the day of salvation.*2Co.6:2 Not some other time—but right now! Not some other day, but this very day!

Isaiah, one of the Old Testament prophets said, *Seek the Lord while He may be found, call upon him while He is near: Let the wicked forsake their ways, and the unrighteous their thoughts: and let them return unto the Lord, and He will have mercy upon them...for He will abundantly pardon.*Is.55:6,7

Prayer

THE LORD IS near you at this very moment, so before you put this book down, if you have not yet accepted Jesus Christ as your personal savior, find a place alone with God where you will not be disturbed. Get on your knees and pray to the Lord this prayer, right out loud:

DEAR LORD, I receive Your gift of eternal life today. I acknowledge that I have sinned against You and that my sins have separated me from You and Your blessing. I am sorry for them, and I truly repent and ask Your forgiveness.

I believe that Jesus Christ died for me, in my place, and rose from the dead to live as my Lord.

I do now welcome You as my savior from sin, from hell, and from all the power of evil. I accept Christ as the Lord of my life.

Lord Jesus, You have said that, if I will come to You, You will in no wise cast me out. I have come to You, seeking salvation and trusting only in Your blood. I know that You do not reject me.

You have said, *If I will confess with my mouth the Lord Jesus, and will believe in my heart that God has raised Him from the dead, I shall be saved.*[Ro.10:9]

I believe with all my heart that You are my Lord, risen from the dead. I do, here and now, confess You as my Master, my savior, my Lord.

Because You died for me, suffering the penalty which I ought to have suffered, I know that my sins can never condemn me again. You paid the full price for my redemption.

You said, *As many as received Him (Jesus Christ), to them He gave the power to become the children of God.*[Jn.1:12]

I believe that You do give me power to become Your child right now. Your blood washes all of my sins and my iniquities away. You were wounded for my transgressions. You were bruised for my iniquities. The punishment I ought to have endured was laid upon You.

From this hour, I will do my best to read some of Your word daily and to please You in all that I think and do and say. I am now a real Christian, a representative of Jesus Christ on earth. I know I am saved. Amen!

Record Your Decision

NOW, AS AN ACT OF FAITH, register your decision by signing your name in the decision box on the next page, and if you are ever influenced to question your salvation, get on your knees, open this book, and read this decision you have made, *out loud*.

MY DECISION

Today I have read this chapter on *The Biblical Christian*. I have learned what it means to be saved. I have sincerely taken the steps outlined here and have reverently prayed the prayer.

I have received Jesus Christ in my life. I am a new creature. I commit my life to do my best to please God in all that I think and say and do. With His grace and help, I shall share Jesus Christ with others.

Relying on Him to keep me by His grace, I have made this decision today, in Jesus' name.

Signed _____

Date _____

Chapter 31

The Mission of Christianity

THE MISSION of Christianity is to witness of Christ and of His resurrection to *all the world*, to *every creature* Mk.16:15 The Apostle Paul was consumed with this passion.

He said, *Whoever shall call on the name of the Lord shall be saved* Ro.10:13 if they *believe in their heart that God raised Jesus from the dead, and if they confess Him as their Lord.* Ro.10:9-10

Then Paul asked the pivotal questions that characterize *The Mission of Christianity.*

How shall they call on him in whom they have not believed? and how shall they believe in him of whom they have not heard? and how shall they hear without a preacher? and how shall they preach except they be sent? Ro.10:14-15

The worldwide ministry that Dr. Daisy, my late wife, and I shared for over five decades, has particularized *The **Mission** of Christianity*, demonstrating for over a half-century the passion and commitment that motivated Paul in his unrelent-ing quest to bring the light of the gospel to those who lived in darkness.

To encourage young men and women with God's call upon their lives, we have included a *brief* on this world ministry that has reached mil-lions for Christ in over eighty nations.

For some mysterious reason God chose Dr. Daisy and me to pioneer the apostolic ministry of *Mass Miracle Evangelism* in *non*-Christian nations. It had not been practiced since the early years of Christianity.

Having gone to India as missionaries in 1945 and having been unable to convince Moslems and Hindus about Christ, we realized that *people must have proof of the gospel and evidence that Jesus is alive.* Not knowing about miracles at that time, we returned to our nation dismayed but not dis-suaded. We believed that, as in Jesus' day and as in the Early Church, the manifestation of signs, miracles and wonders is the only way to demon-strate the power of the gospel of Christ to non-Christians.

*Jesus of Nazareth [himself] was...**approved of God** among people by **miracles** and **wonders** and **signs**, which God did by him in the midst of the people.*^{Ac.2:22}

The Lord mercifully guided us through our di-lemma. Christ appeared to us and we discovered the Bible truths that built into our hearts faith for miracles today. That totally changed the course of our lives.

This pacesetting ministry, pioneering *Mass Miracle Evangelism* among *non*-Christian nations, began back in the era of *Colonial domination* of so-called *Third World* nations. We continued in vast open air campaigns, addressing audiences of from 20,000 to 300,000, through the dangerous years of *Nationalism* and rejection of foreign domination.

Because of the apostolic example of this ministry in action, tens of thousands of national men and women have arisen with fresh faith and have become great gospel ministers to the UNreached and distinguished Christian leaders in many nations of the world.

I am thankful to be able to say that, even in my advancing years, this world ministry continues unabated in this 21st Century as our programs and concepts continue to make an unprecedented impact in this generation.

I am thankful that the anointed ministry of our daughter, Dr. LaDonna Osborn, has become such a leading force in this world ministry. Her preaching, teaching and miracle ministries are rapidly expanding, not only in world evangelism but also in international church leadership at home and abroad.

Daisy Marie Washburn and I were married in Los Banos, California, April 5, 1942 at the ages of 17 and 18. We were missionaries in India at the young ages of 20 and 21. In 1949 we instituted the organization, *The Voice Of Faith Ministry*, later re-named *Osborn Foundation*, and finally code named, *OSFO International*.

Our life passion has been: *To express and propagate the Gospel of Jesus Christ to all people throughout the world.* Our maxim: *No one deserves to hear the Gospel repeatedly until everyone has heard it once.* Our motto: *One Way–Jesus; One Job—Evangelism.* Our guiding principle: *Every Christian believer—a witness for Christ.*

During more than a half-century, Daisy and I proclaimed the Gospel *together* to millions, face to face, in seventy-three nations of the world. Our crusade audiences consistently numbered from twenty-five thousand to over three hundred thousand people.

Dr. Daisy passed away in 1995, but the arms of this ministry continue. Our daughter, Dr. La-Donna shares the preaching, ministry to the sick, and the teaching in our Mass Miracle Crusades and Miracle-Life Seminars. As CEO and Vice-President of *OSFO International*, her expertise is making possible the expansion of this ministry into many new fields as we focus on Russia, French-speaking Africa, East Europe and China.

We have inaugurated numerous plans to reach the UNreached. One program alone has already sponsored over thirty-thousand national preachers as full time missionaries, to their own and neighboring tribes and villages which were previously UNtouched by the gospel.

Our Gospel literature has been published in a hundred and thirty-two languages. Our many *docu*-miracle crusade films, audio and video cassettes, and Bible courses for study and for public evangelism, have been produced in some seventy major languages.

We have provided airlifts and huge shipments of soulwinning tools for Gospel missions and Christian workers worldwide.

We have furnished scores of four-wheel drive mobile vehicles equipped with films, projectors, screens, generators, public-address systems, audio cassettes and cassette players, and enormous quantities of literature in a hundred and thirty-two languages, for evangelism worldwide.

Daisy and I have both disciplined ourselves to carve out the time needed to write the truths that have affected our lives so that they could be shared with millions of people to whom we could never minister in person.

Dr. Daisy's five major books are unprecedented in Christian literature. Her positive writing style is focused to help women discover their **identity**,

dignity, equality, priority and destiny in God's redemptive plan.

Back in 1951 I wrote the book, *Healing the Sick*. It has penetrated the world and is now in its enlarged 45th edition. The publisher calls it *A Living Classic*. It has been a faith-building best-seller since 1951. Over a million copies are in print.

Together, we wrote our 512 page *Classic Documentary* entitled, *The Gospel According To T.L. and Daisy*, (a pictorial world report on our ministries). Nothing else like it has ever been published.

It is commonly reported that we have probably reached and lead more souls to Christ *in non-Christian nations*, and may have witnessed more healing miracles among those multitudes, than any couple in history. That is very humbling, and is certainly not because of superior faith, but simply because we began our ministry so young, and consistently proclaimed the gospel to such vast audiences in so many nations for so many years.

Dr. LaDonna Osborn and the Gospel Torch

Our daughter, Dr. LaDonna Osborn, now carries the *Torch of the Gospel* into this century's new frontiers like China, Russia and East Europe.

Her heritage is certainly unique. She has been engaged in world evangelism from her childhood and her life's passion is to share the Good News of Christ with both women and men of all nations and cultures.

She was conceived in *Calcutta, India* and was born in *Portland, Oregon, USA*. The first Mass Miracle Crusades that she remembers were *Kingston, Jamaica* and *Ponce, Puerto Rico in 1949*.

She learned to speak Spanish in *Camaguey, Cuba* in 1951 and her schooling began in *Barquisimeto, Venezuela* in 1952. Jesus became LaDonna's personal Savior when she was seven years old in *Santiago, Chile* in 1953. Her first missionary journey by boat was from *Argentina, S. America* to *Jakarta, Java, Indonesia* in 1954 and the first lepers she saw miraculously healed were in *Jakarta* and *Surabaya* that same year.

LaDonna was baptized in the Holy Spirit in the *USA* in 1955 and was called to Gospel ministry in *Bangkok, Thailand* in 1956. She gave her first sermon in *Ghana, W. Africa* in 1956. She was baptized in water by Gypsy pastors in *Rennes, France* in 1958 and learned to drive a car in *The Hague, Holland* in 1958.

Her first memories of demonic deliverances through Christ's power were in *Togo, W. Africa* in 1959. Her first recording and photo assignment in God's work was in *Cairo, Egypt, Zambia, Zimbabwe,* and *South Africa* in 1961. She was married in *Birmingham, England* in 1963 after which both she and her husband have ministered with us in many nations.

In 1987, the Lord visited LaDonna, calling her to pastoral ministry and on January 9, 1989, she became the official pastor of Tulsa's *Int'l Gospel Center*. As she has led the church, her focus has been on winning the lost, then on building each convert into effective witnesses for Christ. That dual mission has shaped her life and ministry in a way that combines her world evangelism ministry with her international church leadership.

LaDonna personifies the dual image that Christ gave to His Church; 1) To bring people to Jesus — (*Evangelism*), and 2) To teach people to continue the work of Jesus — (*Equipping*).

As a world evangelist, Dr. LaDonna's passion to help people discover their purpose in Christ *drives her to the remote corners of the earth* where she preaches and teaches with clarity, boldness, and miracle confirmation.

As a pastor, her passion to build people into dedicated representatives for Christ *drives her in a life-changing ministry of teaching the truths of Redemption* that lift believers to their full potential in Christ.

As bishop of more than 200 pastors and churches, her passion is to help Christian leaders grasp God's vision for their world. *This drives her in apostolic leadership that is seeding new life and biblical action in churches at home and abroad.*

Bishop LaDonna's unique style and broad world view are sought after as significant gifts to the Body of Christ, challenging the Church to *BE CHRIST'S BODY IN ACTION — Out Where The People Are.*

In addition to being Vice President and CEO of *OSFO International,* the world missionary institution that we founded in 1949, LaDonna is founder and bishop of the *International Gospel Center Fellowship of Churches and Ministries,* with its headquarters in Tulsa, Oklahoma. She is also a member of the *College of Bishops* for the *International Communion of Charismatic Churches,* representing over ten million believers, spanning every continent.

Dr. LaDonna's classic teaching on *Redemption* is considered the most practical and significant material for grounding new believers and for training Church leaders in the *Dynamics of Christ-Centered Ministry.*

Wherever she ministers, physical healing miracles distinguish her ministry and demonstrate Christ's living presence with her.

Her presentation of the *all encompassing Bible message of the gospel has become the hallmark of her ministry* — both among the masses and within the Church — at home and abroad. Like the Apostle

Paul, she says, *I am not ashamed of the gospel of Christ, for it is the power of God to salvation to everyone who believes.*[Ro.1:16]

Bishop LaDonna's role in *21st Century Church Leadership* is a modern day continuation of apostolic ministry, modeling the necessary balance of evangelism and of discipline—of soulwinning and of training.

She is a prophetic voice reminding the Church and its leaders that *its mission is to share the message of Christ with all people of the world.* She believes that every soul won to Christ must be drawn into the local church where they can grow in God's grace and be trained for Christ-centered ministry.

Dr. LaDonna says: *The World is the Heart of the Church. And the Church is the Hope of the World. The passion of Christ that took Him to the cross is the passion of Christ that continues through the Church*

She contends that without the *World*, the *Church is meaningless* and without the *Church*, the *World is hopeless*.

EVANGELISM: As LaDonna's world ministry compounds, she is keenly aware that the *Gospel Torch* carried by her brave parents for over a half-century *shall continue to be carried throughout the world.*

A WOMAN OF GOD: *As a woman,* LaDonna is determined that the *Gospel Torch* shall be carried more bravely than ever by the royal daughters in God's family. *She personifies a woman of God that will never be limited by archaic Church tradition* and her example is, therefore, pacesetting and inspiring for women around the world.

CHURCH LEADERSHIP: As she functions in her distinguished role of church leadership, she is aware of her unique heritage and *is committed to sharing the secrets she has learned through her decades of ministry with us. Her passion is to impart this vital knowledge with pastors and leaders everywhere, helping them to grasp God's perspective of our hurting world and how to convince non-Christians about Jesus Christ.*

Dr. LaDonna knows the ministry of World Evangelism. She has lived on the front lines from the days of *Colonialism,* through the turbulent years of *Nationalism,* and into this century of *National Church Growth* when the largest churches on earth are being raised up by national pastors in what has been previously referred to as *"Mission Fields."*

As Bishop of over 200 pastors and churches, and as a member of *The College of Bishops* that oversees over ten million church members that span every continent, her spiritual insight and biblical knowledge combines to make her Redemptive teaching not only apostolic and biblical but dynamic in its influence on pastors, leaders and gospel workers.

When dates can be synchronized, LaDonna ministers with me in *Mass Miracle Crusades* and *Miracle Life Seminars*. She shares the crusade preaching, the ministry to the sick and the *Seminar teaching, bringing new faith, hope, love and LIFE to thousands of church leaders, pastors, Bible School students and gospel workers around the world.*

This ministry with its international influence and its arsenal of soulwinning tools and programs, is resolved that the people of Century 21 shall know...1) that the Bible is as valid today as it ever was, 2) that the mission of every believer is to win the lost to Christ, 3) that every soul won can become Christ's representative, and 4) that miracles, signs and wonders will continue to be what distinguishes Christianity from being just another religion.

These issues constitute the essence of
The MISSION of Christianity.

ACTION Ideas

....
....
....
....
....
....
....
....
....
....
....
....
....
....
....
....
....
....
....
....
....
....
....
....

You have not chosen me but I have chosen you, and ordained you, that you should go and bring forth fruit, and that your fruit should remain: that whatever you shall ask of the Father in my name, he may give it you. Jn.15:16

ACTION Results

....
....
....
....
....
....
....
....
....
....
....
....
....
....
....
....
....
....
....
....
....
....
....
....
....
....
....

As many as received Jesus Christ, to them he gave power to become the children of God, even to them that believe on his name. Jn.1:12

INTERNATIONAL DISTRIBUTOR

of Osborn Books.

ACCESS INTERNATIONAL
P.O. Box 700143,
Tulsa, OK 74170-0143 USA

❖❖❖

FRENCH DISTRIBUTORS

Assoc. IMPACT PLEIN EVANGILE
32140 Panassac, France

▫ ▫ ▫

VIE ABONDANTE, B.P. 241,
03208 Vichy, Cedex France

❖❖❖

GERMAN PUBLISHER

SHALOM — VERLAG
Pachlinger Strrasse 10
D-93486 Runding, CHAM, Germany

❖❖❖

PORTUGUESE PUBLISHER

GRACA EDITORIAL
Caixa Postal 1815
Rio de Janiero–RJ–20001, Brazil

❖❖❖

SPANISH PUBLISHER

LIBROS DESAFIO, Apdo. 29724
Bogota, Colombia

❖❖❖

(For Quantity Orders, Request Discount Prices.)